THE DISAPPEARING IRISH COTTAGE:
A CASE-STUDY OF NORTH DONEGAL

The disappearing Irish cottage:
a case-study of north Donegal

Clive Symmons and Seamus Harkin

Wordwell

First published in 2004 by
Wordwell Ltd
PO Box 69, Bray, Co. Wicklow
www.wordwellbooks.com

Library of Congress Cataloging-in-Publication Data are available for this
book.

A CIP catalogue record for this book is available from the British Library.

ISBN 1869857 78 X

This publication has received support from the Heritage Council under
the 2004 Publications Grant Scheme.

Cover design: Rachel Dunne

Copy-editing: Emer Condit

Typesetting and layout: Wordwell Ltd

Book design: Nick Maxwell, Andrew Gregory, Rachel Dunne

Printed by E.G. Zure S.A., Bilbao

CONTENTS

FOREWORD

The subject-matter of this study is the fate of vernacular Irish dwellings. Such dwellings may loosely be described as 'cottages', as in the title of this book, although a more accurate description might be 'longhouse'. Both terms are used interchangeably here. Although this study is essentially regional in emphasis (north Donegal), the fate of such dwellings is, in the authors' opinion, a matter of national concern, if not scandal. Large numbers of these former 'jewels' of the Irish countryside are disappearing yearly, so that few now exist even as ruins. Sadly, in some cases the misguided planning policies of local authorities and the past lack of any conservation provisions have hastened their demise, particularly with the controversial advent of 'bungalow bliss' and one-off building in the Irish countryside, which is, in effect, the other side of the coin.

In an ideal world, this study would have been carried out at least twenty years ago to record what in such a short time has been lost for ever. For it is unlikely that the time-consuming structural methods of the past—and the mining and preparation of local materials such as flags and slates—will ever reoccur; so that, for example, a slate roof deliberately removed, or which has collapsed through neglect, is most likely gone for ever. The Irish countryside is undoubtedly the worse for this process, and in time, if not already, it will impact adversely on the tourist industry: the 'Irish cottage' that features in the famous John Hinde photographs is now very hard to find in the rural parts of Ireland. It is, therefore, the aim of this small study to tell, with photographic evidence, a tale which could be replicated in any part of the Atlantic fringe of Ireland, recording what little remains of this important part of Irish tradition before it is finally lost. We hope that it may prick the consciences of officialdom and others to act to save this vital part of our heritage.

In conducting this study the authors have tried to seek permission for photography of vernacular buildings and contents, but as time was limited it was not always possible to discover who the owners might be. In such cases and where the cottage was obviously derelict — often with the door flapping in the breeze or missing — in the interests of research some liberties were taken with the laws of trespass, and the authors can only plead 'Forgive us our trespasses'! In any event, to preserve the privacy of the current owners of such vernacular dwellings, the names of townlands, owners, etc., have generally been omitted. Apologies are also made in advance to the owners of modern replacements of former cottages for any implicit criticism which emerges over planning policies in County Donegal; our sole aim has been to highlight the perceived problem of conservation, and we hope that such owners will accept our remarks in this spirit.

We would like to thank all the local people (such as Rita McCarry) who facilitated this study and whose cottages appear in it — and who, in some cases, agreed to be photographed and interviewed. We would also like to thank the photographic unit of the History of Art Department at Trinity College Dublin — including Ruth Sheehy and Ann Crookshank — for processing many of the photographs; Freddie Symmons for inserting the numerous illustrative photographs digitally into the original text; Eddie McPartland and Fidelma Mullane for reading the text; Joe Gallagher (Heritage Officer for Donegal CC) for his friendly assistance in supplying additional sources of reading; Nick Maxwell of Wordwell for his unfailing enthusiasm and encouragement; and not least the Heritage Council for their generous grant to assist publication.

THE AUTHORS

Seamus Harkin

Local history and folklore have always been part of Seamus Harkin's life. He grew up in a rural area where everyone knew their neighbours for miles around. As a child he listened to his father and grandfather, who both had a vast store of knowledge, telling the stories of the happenings around the Creeslough and Dunfanaghy area. Then, travelling the countryside as an insurance salesman for fourteen years, he got to know all the houses in that area. With the knowledge he acquired in the course of his work, coupled with the information he received from his forefathers, he has been able to gather a valuable amount of local history. In recent years he has recorded some of that folklore in a book about the poets and people of his parish, entitled *Poets and people of Doe*.

Clive Symmons

Dr Clive Symmons is a research fellow at Trinity College Dublin and Adjunct Professor of Law at NUI, Galway. He has long had an interest in the conservation of vernacular rural buildings, particularly since he purchased a derelict old cottage in north Donegal in the early 1970s. Since then he has had 'hands-on' experience in restoring this cottage, as well as an old watermill in County Meath, where he currently lives. He has been an active member of the An Taisce Vernacular Buildings Committee and is currently chairman of Mills and Millers of Ireland, an association dedicated to the preservation and conservation of old mill buildings.

Map showing area of study (after the Royal Irish Academy's *Atlas of Ireland* (Dublin, 1979)).

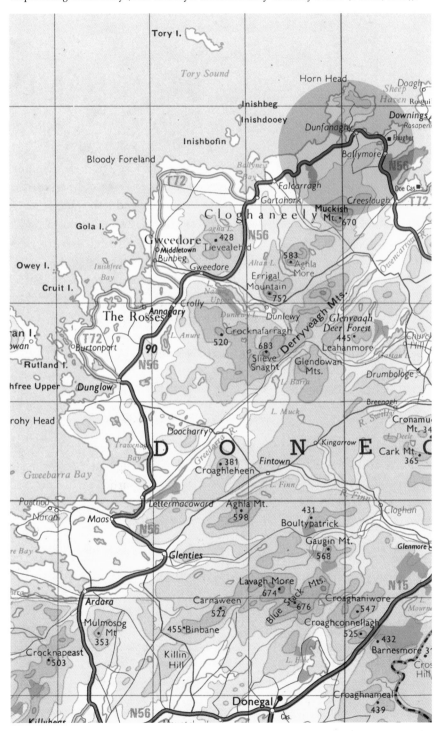

INTRODUCTION

The aim of this study is to fill a gap in the existing literature[1] by looking at what now remains of the traditional type of rural vernacular buildings (including the types of outbuildings that were associated with such dwellings in a farming context) in an area of north Donegal around Dunfanaghy (mostly contained in Donegal OS sheets 25 and 26—see map on page ix)—an area broadly categorised as 'Landscape Category 2' under the Material Alteration (No. 1) to the Draft County Donegal Development Plan of 1998.

It is generally accepted that only detailed fieldwork can properly record the charming characteristics of such a humble architectural style,[2] and that is just what has been attempted in this particular study, where in general only the more typical one-storey type of vernacular building ('longhouse') has been looked at and is discussed in the text.

It is perhaps worth stating just what the term 'vernacular' generally implies. A recent—but somewhat geographically broader—study in Northern Ireland[3] has aptly listed for its survey of rural vernacular buildings the following characteristics (all of which can be seen in the Dunfanaghy district examples, as will be discussed):

- built without benefit of any special plan (i.e. not formally designed);
- linear rectangular construction;
- depth normally limited by roof construction to about 6m;
- walls of mass load-bearing materials;
- chimneys always located along the ridge line;
- the front door opening directly into the kitchen, which had a hearth and solid floor;
- opes (door and window) normally on the front or rear wall (i.e. not on gable ends), of relatively small proportions and often unsymmetrical;
- any extension carried out in a linear direction, except possibly for the addition of a small front-door windbreak or porch;
- a set relationship between roof pitch and height of building;
- internal transverse walls that extended to the roof apex and were load-bearing.

Some 40 years ago in the Dunfanaghy area single-storey vernacular buildings ('longhouses') fitting such descriptions were abundant and many were still lived in, though even then several were in ruins. Today very few remain intact, most having been either demolished or allowed to fall into ruin [Pl. 1a–d]. A recent survey in Northern Ireland[4] shows how

1

Pl. 1a—The 'footprint'—last remnants of a small cottage in Kildarragh.

Pl. 1b—The ruined shell of a long-abandoned cottage in Roshine.

Pl. 1c—Another roofless shell.

Pl. 1d—One of several ruins now used as cattle shelters.

dramatic the loss of rural vernacular buildings has been there: 49% of those existing in 1909 have completely gone, 39% have been altered (often beyond recognition), and only 12% remain intact. It has not been possible in the present survey to give such statistics for the Donegal study area, though they would probably be similar.

There can be no doubt that such 'longhouses'[5] [Pl. 2a–b] have added a wonderful scenic dimension to the north Donegal countryside. Moreover, as Pfeiffer and Shaffrey note, such vernacular buildings, 'humble as they are, are not only lovely in themselves but are also a significant part of [Irish] social history';[6] and, in the writers' opinion, it is certainly true that they 'sit comfortably among their surroundings in a way that their modern counterpart, the bungalow, which has spread so rapidly in Ireland . . . , never will'.[7] The reason for this is that, unlike the ubiquitous bungalow, 'the older type of house was in right harmony with its surroundings'.[8] Estyn Evans in his famous book *Irish folk ways*[9] explains why these rural houses look so good in the Irish countryside: 'The use of local building materials meant that they fitted into landscapes of which they were literally a part, their clay or stone walls gathered from the earth on the spot, their timbers gathered from the bogs, their thatch harvested from the fields'. In this sense of being constructed from truly local building materials—stone, earth, sods, slates, grasses, rushes etc.—the Donegal cottages can in a very real way be described as 'vernacular'. In addition, their small-scale construction harmonises perfectly with the Donegal landscape. Such qualities are lacking in the proliferation of modern houses which now have the potential to scar the landscape of County Donegal and elsewhere. As Michael Viney has aptly commented, what is missing in the case of present rural planning is 'any sense of connection between the house and its natural setting, any resonance with the forms and materials of the landscape, the palpable regime of its weather, or even its human history'.[10]

Sadly, the sentimental musings of past writers on the vernacular aspect of the Irish rural landscape—such as that (even in the 1980s) throughout Donegal 'sparkling white cottages dot the landscape'[11]—now have a historical ring to them, even if as recently as the 1950s (in the Irish countryside generally) one could '[f]rom some elevated position in the mountainy parts . . . count hundreds of small whitewashed homesteads dotted among the fields, each nestling behind a handful of wind-bent trees and approached by its own access road— . . . the borheen' and defended by a gate hung between 'stout stone gate pillars'.[12] The situation

Pl. 2a—One of the longer local cottages still in good repair and now used as a holiday home.

Pl. 2b—The cottage of one of the authors in Roshine before final conservation work (the byre door to right is now a window to a sitting room).

Pl. 3a—The ruin of one of the smallest cottages in the area; originally it would have been thatched.

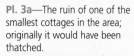

Pl. 3b—One of the surviving 'children' of the family that once lived in the cottage inside his old front door!

today is that only a handful of such cottages still remain in the area of this study (and indeed in other parts of County Donegal). Quite apart from the heritage aspect, such a loss of traditional cottages can only have an adverse effect on tourism in the county.[13] The reasons for this irreversible tragedy for the Donegal landscape are not hard to find.

Firstly, local people have in the recent past tended to look down upon, and even to despise, these humble dwellings that in their day have housed large families within their walls, so that '[d]eep-rooted folk memories of the harsh conditions in which our ancestors lived have . . . undoubtedly led to many cottages being abandoned or altered almost beyond recognition'.[14] Allied to this may be a sense of apathy and the loss of the old skills necessary to maintain this vernacular building tradition.[15] Strangely enough, however, in interviewing local Donegal folk for this study, the authors found that most of the older interviewees seemed to have predominantly happy memories of their now-abandoned houses, crowded and damp though they may have been. In one of the older cottages, for example, in one townland—a tiny two-roomed thatched dwelling—twelve children, two parents and a grandparent shared a bedroom measuring only about 9ft long by 12ft wide [Pl. 3a–b]! This figure beggars belief, but one of the remaining 'children' assured the authors that despite the cramped conditions he never once caught the 'flu!

Undoubtedly, though, the folk memory association with past poverty has prompted many local people to abandon such dwellings in the Donegal countryside and to opt for 'bungalow bliss'. This mentality has been particularly evident amongst the younger generation, who would view the traditional Donegal cottage layout—with interconnecting rooms and no corridors—as impracticable for modern living or might believe that such old cottages, draughty and damp as they can be, are incapable of conversion to modern standards of living. However, there is no reason why such past inconveniences and problems should not be overcome at a moderate cost by the tasteful use of modern building techniques such as damp-proofing;[16] indeed, one or two cottages in the study area have been modernised in this manner in complete sympathy with their vernacular style, albeit as holiday homes[17] [Pl. 4a–b]. Herein lies the irony that most of the 'rescued' cottages of north Donegal are now owned by 'blow-ins' (such as one of the present authors), including several Continentals, who do appreciate the worth of such old buildings. The pity is that at present conservation grants for restoring and updating such old buildings are virtually non-existent[18] and that not all councils yet have full-time

Pl. 4a—A cottage in Roshine tastefully converted into a holiday home with all modern conveniences.

Pl. 4b—The former owner of the above cottage, with his donkey harnessed to a cart.

Pl. 5a—The view as it once was looking towards the heights of Horn Head, with donkeys in the foreground and an isolated old cottage to the left. Just to the left of the road in this photo there now stands a 'Dallas-type' modern house complete with satellite dish!

Pl. 5b—The same road with the last working donkeys in the area bringing home the turf.

conservation/heritage officers to keep a check on the fate of such buildings.[19] However, in November 2002 Donegal County Council advertised for (and subsequently appointed) a heritage officer for its own county; and in 2004 a conservation officer was appointed in the county to oversee the fate of old buildings.[20] Despite these developments, it seems that none of the vernacular buildings mentioned in this survey has been listed on the latest County Donegal recommended Record of Protected Structures (as of summer 2004).[21]

A second—and perhaps more worrying—reason for the decline of vernacular buildings in the study area is that the county planners themselves have not appeared in the past to appreciate the architectural and cultural worth of such old rural dwellings, which are now widely interspersed with inappropriate modern buildings [Pl. 5a–b]. Far from ensuring their preservation, it appears that the planners have—in the past, at any rate—been actively bringing about their destruction. One reason for this is that in scenic parts of County Donegal the only way of getting planning permission may have been to own a site with an old cottage on it (not even necessarily ruinous)—as opposed to a 'greenfield' site—and to be given planning permission for a new bungalow on condition of bulldozing the old dwelling and building anew on its site [Pl. 6a–d].[22] The authors view this past aspect of the planning process as amounting to official encouragement to destroy part of Donegal's vernacular past,[23] but hopefully it will be over-ridden in the current County Development Plan, one objective of which is to achieve refurbishment of derelict or run-down vernacular buildings by holiday home-owners where they would not get planning permission for a new building. It is also to be hoped that with the new planning and conservation legislation coming into effect[24] this sort of wilful destruction will cease and that even such few humble dwellings as survive will be included in the list of 'protected structures' under the new listing process, irrespective of whether they are now in a ruinous state.[25] According to information received from Donegal County Council, the council engaged consultants to prepare a draft record of 'protected structures' in 2002. These consultants concluded that the current Dúchas draft inventory for the county was too limited in respect of geographic coverage and typology of structures, particularly regarding vernacular buildings. The council subsequently published a draft record of protected structures in 2003.

Sadly, however, it may turn out that the humble vernacular cottages will have least priority in any listing process, if only because their sites are

Pl. 6a—One of the former most beautiful cottages on Horn Head (once much painted by local artists!), roofed then in local slates and with thatched outbuildings.

Pl. 6b—The same cottage complex, showing its spectacular position overlooking Dunfanaghy.

Pl. 6c—The beginning of the end: the original slated roof has been stripped and replaced with tin and an ugly modern window has replaced the small sash one.

Pl. 6d—The same site as it is today.

less well known than other historic buildings[26] and their preservation seems not to have been a priority in the planning process generally [Pl. 7a–c]. This factor has been acknowledged in Donegal County Council's recent publication, entitled *Record of Protected Structures: response and recommendations to submissions made during the public consultation process.* This report, whilst accepting that the Donegal 'built' heritage included 'vernacular cottages', admitted that 'buildings which are of local importance have not been recorded on the [Draft Record of Protected Structures] at this time'. In consequence none of the cottages mentioned in this study has so far been included in the processed list.

It was for such reasons that one of the authors submitted to Donegal County Council a detailed account of the cottages in the Dunfanaghy region that should, in his opinion, be listed, complete with Ordnance Survey map references. This was in response to an advertisement published by the council relating to a draft inventory of architectural heritage for County Donegal (prepared on behalf of Dúchas), under which the council undertook early in 2001 to carry out a public consultation process to create public awareness of the inventory and to get public feedback, particularly on potential 'listing' gaps, whether as to geographic locations or building types.[27]

The ongoing problem of the demolition of such existing buildings to make way for modern bungalows (often, in the past at any rate, aided and abetted by the planning process itself) can be seen in the instance of a local cottage that one of the authors has long admired[28] [Pl. 6a–d]—a marvellous traditional cottage that until recently overlooked the town of Dunfanaghy on the ascending heights of Horn Head, an area of great natural beauty. Ironically, as recently as the early '90s this cottage was singled out by Pfeiffer and Shaffrey[29] as one of the exemplars of Irish cottages on an *all-Ireland* basis and merited its own colour photo in their book. Today it is totally demolished and a modern two-storey structure stands in its place; but even before this happened progressive destruction of its vernacular character was evident, most particularly in the stripping of the main roof—its locally quarried ('Roshine') slates being replaced by naked 'tin' (unpainted corrugated iron sheeting)—and the ripping out of the old vernacular windows. In this one case the authors happen to have a complete photographic history of the fate of the cottage, so that the extent of this loss can be appreciated in full. But this example can be multiplied many times over, for other recent examples can be found everywhere in the study area [Pl. 7a–c].

9

Pl. 7a—The view as it once was in an area of Horn Head looking towards the (then) cottage below (Pl. 7b).

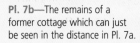

Pl. 7b—The remains of a former cottage which can just be seen in the distance in Pl. 7a.

Pl. 7c—The large new building which now stands on the site of the former cottage.

Thirdly, wilful or benign neglect—largely owing to lack of local appreciation—is another common fate of old cottages in County Donegal,[30] where surviving examples are usually in a ruinous state. Thus one often sees in north Donegal an old dwelling-house left standing in the background of the 'bungalow bliss' replacement and now thought fit only for use as an extra byre [Pl. 8a–c] or surrounded by applications for planning permission [Pl. 9a–b].

Fourthly, misguided 'modernisation', without proper conservation protection, has meant that many of the surviving Donegal cottages have been changed beyond all recognition under the guise of upgrading an old property[31] [Pl. 10a] or subjected to the use of inappropriate non-vernacular materials [Pl. 10b]. This can happen very suddenly; recently one of the authors revisited a site in a local townland to photograph what had been a lovely example of an old cottage with a hayloft, only to find that the original (Roshine) slates of the main house had just previously been replaced by synthetic modern ones, and that the adjacent hayloft had been demolished to make way for a garage constructed of concrete blocks [Pl. 11a]! It is to be hoped that the above-mentioned current Donegal County Development Plan will take such 'modernisation' factors into account when granting permission for the 'refurbishment' of old buildings.

Pl. 8a— A well-sited cottage in Derryreel (now used as a byre).

Pl. 8b—An old cottage near Port now used for farm purposes.

Pl. 8c—An old cottage—with its former porch recently removed —now used for farm purposes.

THE TYPICAL VERNACULAR RURAL DWELLING OF NORTH DONEGAL

The typical rural vernacular buildings that are discussed in this study have been aptly described as extended 'linear' houses, usually, as will be seen, single-storey.[32] They evolved slowly through time up to the latter part of the nineteenth century.

Size and shape

Set width

As Gailey says, 'All vernacular houses in Ireland share some fundamental characteristics', being generally 'a single room deep between front and rear walls', with each room thus running to the full width of the house, usually between twelve and fifteen feet.[33] Such vernacular, linear-style houses ('longhouses'), deriving from 'ancient origins', were rectangular in plan, the 'one-room-deep' width being determined by the length of available roof timbers.[34] As in centuries past lengthy timber was scarce—as were trees generally (see below)—the builders of the day had to make do with moderate lengths of wood, such as bog timber. Thus Irish cottages might grow in length—as is so typical in north Donegal—and sometimes in height but never in depth. The vernacular tradition insisted on 'lengthwise extension of the dwelling at ground level'.[35] Indeed, there seems to have been a superstitious reason for this pattern. As Estyn Evans notes,[36] 'The long rectangular shape was sanctioned by custom and preserved by superstition: a house to be "lucky" must not be more than one room wide'; so that typically—as will be seen in greater detail below—any extension was lengthwise.[37]

Small size: the primitive 'byre' cottage

What have been referred to as 'byre-dwellings'—the 'most basic form' of humble dwelling[38]—were widely used in Donegal, particularly in the far north-west,[39] in the early nineteenth century. These dwellings were so called because they offered no physical separation between the byre (containing, for example, cattle) and the living accommodation—apart, perhaps, from a (stone-lined) drain (to get rid of the animal effluent) or a flagged walkway running through the base of the front or rear byre wall, according to the slope[40]—so that cattle (and all that goes with them[41]) and humans co-existed under the same roof.[42] Hence the old rhyme: 'at one of

Pl. 9a—A once-lovely cottage (sadly damaged by fire) with a planning application to its front and a modern bungalow close to its side.

Pl. 9b—The same cottage—how long will it survive?

Pl. 10a—An old cottage in Roshine which has, in the past, been 'modernised' with cement external rendering and use of asbestos slates.

Pl. 10b—An old cottage in the process of being modernised (with a large roof-light inserted into the Roshine slates).

the ends he [the cottage-dweller] kept his cows, and at the other end he kept his spouse'.[43] Estyn Evans comments[44] that in fact many dwellings along the Atlantic seaboard were not 'far removed from kitchen-byres', a cross-partition conveniently converting the byre into a bedroom, store or dairy. Living conditions in such early dwellings were undoubtedly harsh. Estyn Evans recounts[45] how in a single-room Irish byre-house at the end of the eighteenth century the family would sleep naked on the floor in front of the fire; and he relates that in Donegal, even in the nineteenth century, sons and daughters would sleep together on the floor 'in bare buff'. It seems that this forerunner of the well-known Irish cottage began to be confined to the Irish west coast and mountainous districts by the mid-nineteenth century. However, the 1841 census showed high percentages of one-roomed cottages throughout west Donegal.[46]

Gailey[47] says that '[t]ypically, the byre-dwelling was about 9m long, 5 to 5.5m wide, and solidly constructed with stone walls 0.6m thick, sometimes built dry, sometimes mortared'. The roof would typically have been covered by locally available materials—for example, as in the Dunfanaghy region, the rough but beautiful 'Roshine' slate, or thatch made of local grasses such as mountain grass, rushes or sea grass.

The authors tried without success to find an existing example of such a 'byre-cottage' in the study area, although several small ruined or deserted dwellings may in their heyday have been of this type [Pl. 11b].

Extensions lengthways over time

It appears that over time such single-room dwellings were changed by partitioning off the byre end[48] and/or by adding to the original edifice in a linear fashion, often comprising two or three extra rooms in a row,[49] each room being a simple rectangle of from 10ft to 20ft long. In time, such a building became more like the aptly named 'longhouse' by progressive elongation[50] and (as seen above) never by widening. Of the built units, one would typically have provided the 'principal living space' (a kitchen), with other units being added to provide 'sleeping quarters', but all under one roof with—if byres were also added—separate entrances for humans and cattle.[51]

Indeed, in the Dunfanaghy area outbuildings in the form of byres were typically added to the outer extremities, and so further 'separation of man and beast was achieved by building a separate byre with its own external entrance onto the end of the house',[52] or there may also have been an interconnecting internal door to the byre.[53] As a result, the house and

15

Pl. 11a—An old cottage now roofed with modern slates (replacing the old Roshine slates) and with the former adjacent half-loft demolished.

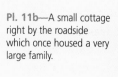 **Pl. 11b**—A small cottage right by the roadside which once housed a very large family.

Pl. 12—A cottage in Roshine where the two chimneys to the left would probably have started off at two gable ends when the house was first built.

associated outbuildings ultimately formed one continuous line, the kitchen/living-room—the most important room in the house[54]—being typically engulfed in the middle of the 'longhouse', with bedrooms at one or both sides. In its most common form the 'longhouse' ultimately had three compartments, with the kitchen placed centrally between two bedrooms (the 'upper' and 'lower' rooms, the lower being where the larger animals were originally housed)[55]—the so-called 'three-purlin' cottage; but sometimes there were just two units.[56] Thus any surviving Donegal 'longhouse' may (as in the case of the cottage of one of the authors) have chimneys now situated (wholly or partially) on the inner roof line of the house, having started off with a chimney (or chimneys) at a formerly exposed gable end[57] [Pl. 12].

In the Dunfanaghy region it was apparently common to have the stable next to the kitchen. One reason for this may have been that the horses liked the heat coming from the party wall containing the fire; another may be that horses were not as smelly as cows. In any event, the horse stamping its foot on the flags of the stable floor was a common sound that reverberated into the kitchen, a memory recalled in a poem by W. F. Marchels: 'the house was like a graveyard bar the mare would give a stamp'. Unusually, in one farmstead there is a narrow unit positioned between living-room and byre under the main roof that was used for housing ducks and hens [Pl. 13]; here again the heat from the living-room fire was popular with the fowl, who apparently laid their eggs in its vicinity!

By the nineteenth century two- and three-unit houses 'with a byre added at one gable became common'.[58] The addition of a byre to one end of the units could be said to help maintain the tradition that 'people and cattle were accommodated under the same roof',[59] though sometimes the incorporated range of outbuildings, even if attached, had separate roof lines (particularly in the case of the commonly featured 'hayloft' at the end) (see below) or existed simply as a 'lean-to' at the end gable.[60] The roofing material—as well as roof ridge heights[61]—could vary in the case of such byre additions, often being a cruder form of material such as rushes or, later, painted 'tin' (corrugated iron) [Pl. 14a–b].

Such stage-by-stage development of vernacular buildings (often, as seen, from one-room cabins or 'byre-houses') may be detected by means of breaks in construction in the walls (i.e. no interlocking stones at each dividing wall) and variations in the roof, whether in covering material[62] or individual ridge-span heights [Pls 2b, 15a–h]. Many of the old

Pl. 13—A cottage with an unusual narrow room (to right-hand side of photo) where chickens were once housed.

Pl. 14a—A typical Donegal cottage with lateral outbuildings and roofs of varying heights (and in some cases roofed with differing materials).

Pl. 14b—A cottage with some 'tin' roofing.

'longhouses' in north Donegal and the Dunfanaghy region show clear signs of having been built in such stages, starting with a one-room dwelling and then spreading left and right, as all room segments are not of interlocking stone [Pl. 16]. This largely accounts for another feature of Donegal (and other Irish) vernacular dwellings, namely that of 'division of interior units separated by load-bearing walls',[63] so that as the interior walls of such buildings extend up to the very roof, each room may be considered almost as a separate unit in its own right,[64] the 'mass' walls—both internal and external—being typically made of local stone in the Dunfanaghy region.

In this way, each unit of these old buildings can be identified by cross-walls rising up to the roof line or even to gables above roof level[65]—one of the hallmarks, as seen, of vernacular architecture (the usual Irish practice being to carry load-bearing walls up to the roof ridge[66]). The possible slight rises and falls of gables may help to indicate the number of rooms in a cottage in the same way as the linear roofs of Donegal outbuildings are often markedly stepped down progressively in height [Pl. 15a–h].

To cater for large families all living under the same roof—and with increasing regard to elements of privacy—what was once a separate byre section could later be converted to living space. In north-west Donegal this started as early as 1840, when landlords gave premiums for separate entrances for man and beast[67] in order to discourage internal byres in dwellings. In addition (see below), a trend started towards partitioning off sections of existing large rooms—such as the kitchen—as separate bedrooms, especially for the females of the household. Thus the traditional separation in County Donegal of the old byre-house and living space came to be diluted by the conversion of a byre into a bedroom,[68] which in fact was easily effected by knocking through an internal door from the existing dwelling rooms and adding new windows as appropriate.

Conversely, it would appear that as family numbers decreased through emigration the living spaces in formerly overcrowded houses might contract, so that, for example, any unit used for sleeping behind and above the hearth wall was abandoned.[69] In this way, in a later reversal of the expansion process, formerly 'reclaimed' byres may have become byres once more.[70] The number of blocked-up internal doorways in the study region indicates that interchangeability of room uses over time was quite common [Pl. 17].

Pl. 15a—Note the steep drop in roof line (to right) in the case of this old cottage.

Pl. 15b—A cottage with only slightly varying roof heights.

Pl. 15c—A cottage complex with progressively descending heights of roof ridges and gables.

Pl. 15d—Another (more modernised) example of progressively descending roof lines.

Age, method of design, building and siting

Age and method of design and building

As the County Donegal vernacular rural buildings were constructed to 'accord with locally accepted tradition'[71] they are difficult to date before the appearance of the earliest Ordnance Survey maps (i.e. before 1834). Many were probably built in the eighteenth and nineteenth centuries, with outbuildings added on later.[72] Construction in accordance with a traditional pattern, and of local materials, imposed a certain uniformity without the necessity for any architectural plans or expertise, and so this popular house form changed only slowly and minimally through time.[73] Furthermore, as non-contemporary timbers—such as very old timbers long preserved in the peat bogs—were often used as roofing beams, dendrochronological methods of dating may be of no help. Nonetheless, the other types of main timbers may still give a rough guide as to the general period of construction.[74] The expert vernacular historian, Gailey, is of the opinion that use of bog timber (so prevalent, as will be seen, in the Dunfanaghy region) may in itself suggest an origin as far back as the eighteenth century.[75]

This traditional consistency of house pattern was reinforced by the fact that the amateur builders of the day were often collaborating in a neighbourly spirit and operating according to handed-down methods of construction. Such communal effort might involve such tasks as gathering stones 'cooperatively'.[76] That famous landlord commentator on west Donegal rural life, Lord George Hill, referred to the pre-Famine custom of using the collective skills of the whole community; it was usual to hire a fiddler and for all the neighbours to cooperate in carrying and assembling the building materials.[77]

In the study area, if a special job had to be done, such as building a byre or sometimes a dwelling-house, it seems that several neighbours would gather for a 'meitheal' (in the Creeslough area) or a 'fruz' (in the Dunfanaghy area). Sometimes the job was done in a day, and this may have led to rushed and haphazard building work in some cases, such as inappropriate and differing heights for doors and window lintels [Pl. 18]. Once the task was completed, a fiddler would be employed to provide music for dancing until daybreak.

As is typical of vernacular architecture generally, it seems that specialists were not employed in house-building in parts of west County Donegal until at least the end of the nineteenth century.[78]

Pl. 15e—Another example of varying roof levels, accentuated here by whitewashed 'wind skews'.

Pl. 15f—A roof-ridge angle photo accentuating the slightly differing segments of roof height.

Pl. 15g—In the case of this cottage, the lower roof lines of the outbuildings accentuate the habitable dwelling in the centre.

Pl. 15h—Another end-on photo which shows the significant change of elevations from one part of the cottage to the other.

Siting

The typical surviving Donegal 'longhouse' is in an isolated, or relatively isolated, position, there having been even since Early Christian times an element in the settlement pattern of 'individual dwellings dispersed over the landscape'.[79] Estyn Evans mentions the rural mentality behind this: namely, the express desire of most country people to have an 'isolated dwelling house',[80] the once-familiar small Irish communal settlement—the 'clachan'—having become despised as a 'symbol of poverty'; so that, for the last century at least, the isolated farm has characterised the Irish rural scene.[81] In some areas, however, Donegal rural dwellings were in clusters (clachans), this being originally associated with infield/outfield rundale operation of farming activities and the exploitation of common pastures; in this arrangement little privacy existed and buildings were often badly sited in relation to each other.[82]

Some of the surviving cottages in the Roshine area near Dunfanaghy form such tight communities of two or more cottages—originally, at least, lived in by separate families—in an almost terraced line with no dividing wall in the 'street' outside. For example, in one Roshine site [Pl. 19a–b] two farm cottages have a dividing space of only some 3ft between them. By all accounts the two women living there for much of the earlier part of the last century in the (then) separate households fell out over disputes about hens and ownership of eggs, so that a 6ft-high dividing wall had to be built to end the arguments![83] More unusually, the cluster could even be in a courtyard shape, as in a farmstead where several separate families once lived [Pl. 20a–b].

Typically in the Dunfanaghy area the cottages are tucked into hillsides,[84] 'shelter from the winds' being the prime consideration in choosing a site[85]—a preference no doubt influenced by the famous 'Big Wind' of 6 January 1839. Thus many of the cottages in the townland of Roshine have been built into a bank behind, sometimes with a back window only just above the bank line! This could, of course, have the unfortunate effect of creating damp, and even, in at least one case, of causing water in exceptional storms to seep in under the back wall and exit in a stream under the front door![86]

A stand of protecting trees in the study area is usually a sure sign of the presence of a cottage;[87] the primary purpose of the trees was again to provide shelter from the wind but they also offered privacy.[88] The favourite tree in the Dunfanaghy region was the sycamore, with its dense foliage and reputation for resistance to salt-laden gales in a coastal area.

Pl. 16—The back of a derelict cottage in Roshine where the separate (and later) construction of outer buildings can be clearly seen in the separate stonework.

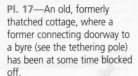

Pl. 17—An old, formerly thatched cottage, where a former connecting doorway to a byre (see the tethering pole) has been at some time blocked off.

Pl. 18—A small ruined cottage in Derryreel with a very low door lintel and wall height.

This feature can be traced back to at least the nineteenth century. Ordnance Survey memoirs from the nineteenth century refer to farmhouses being 'almost hidden from view in clusters of trees'[89] [Pl. 21]. Some cottages, however, in the coastal region of the study area do have exposed positions overlooking the sea [Pl. 22a–b].

To add to the cottage's isolation and privacy, the approach to it was often along a narrow and winding laneway—the 'boreen' [Pl. 23a][90]—the entrance to which is still to this day often announced by impressive rounded stone gate-pillars. These pillars were regularly whitewashed[91] [Pl. 23b].

As regards the siting of farm buildings, in the typical 'longhouse' a separate byre (or byres)—ultimately separate from human living space—was 'usually attached to the house'[92] at one or both ends;[93] and even many small byre-dwellings had 'small outhouses associated with them' as animal shelters and implement stores.[94] These farm buildings were, as discussed above, typically added in linear fashion to the dwelling units at either gable (sometimes in lean-to fashion), and housed the larger domestic animals such as cattle and horses and the farm cart; but they could also be separate from the linear terrace, set out as separate units or in courtyard fashion or parallel to the main buildings[95] [Pl. 19b], particularly in the case of houses for pigs and smaller farm animals such as chickens, ducks and geese (known locally by the Gaelic name *cró*). A separate grain and threshing barn was not unusual [Pl. 24].

In north Donegal it seems that the byre sections of farmhouses were in fact often purposely built into banks of higher ground so that hay etc. could be stored at ground height via an elevated back door and then fed down to the cattle below [Pl. 24], and at the front there were often outside steps up to the hayloft, which might for this purpose have a higher roof than the rest of the linear buildings[96] [Pl. 25].

Size of rooms
The sizes of vernacular houses tend to fall 'within fairly well-defined limits'.[97] In part, of course, this was due to tradition, but there was also a very practical explanation—namely (as discussed above) the availability of building materials, and most particularly timber for roofing. As will be seen, in many cases 'bog timbers' were used as purlins carrying the main spans of the roof, which, whether in terms of limited lengths or, more likely, sheer weight, meant that spans lengthwise tended to average not more than 12–15ft,[98] although they could sometimes be as long as 18ft.

Pl. 19a—Two cottages in Roshine separated by a minimal gap where two different families once lived side by side.

Pl. 19b—The communal 'street' to the above cottages.

Pl. 20a—An unusually concentrated group of human habitations and outbuildings near Port.

Pl. 20b—Sometimes—as in the case of this cottage grouping—different families lived at different ends of the same longhouse!

Internal room sizes in cottages in the study area conform to these dimensions.[99]

Type and method of wall construction
The 'mass' walls of Irish vernacular houses—up to 2ft thick—were often dry-built of roughly coursed rubble or slightly coursed stone, depending on the local source. In the Dunfanaghy region the material is usually local slate-type ('Roshine') stones of various sizes (of the same type as might also constitute roofing material), interspersed with occasional big stones (or layers of larger stones), particularly on the lower courses and gable ends;[100] sometimes just large stones are used [Pl. 26a], or local boulders are simply incorporated at ground level and left projecting [Pl. 26b]. The same Roshine stone—slate slabs or 'flags'—is commonly also used in such cottages as lintels for both doors and windows, as window-sills [Pl. 27a–b] and, as will be seen, as fire lintels and chimney-breasts (a localised feature of the Dunfanaghy area, in the authors' opinion).

Originally stone buildings in the more remote parts of Donegal were normally left unrendered; unmortared drystone walling was used,[101] some of it very artistically constructed [Pl. 28], possibly with, in some cases, lime mortar pointing on the surfaces of external walls and also on the load-bearing internal walls;[102] and even if not applied originally, mortar may have been pushed into the stone joints at a later stage.[103] Such lime plaster on walls allows them to breathe, just like limewash itself. In fact most Donegal cottages seem now to show a thin coating of lime plaster over stone[104] [Pl. 29], but in some cases this may be deceptive as layers of successive limewashes (applied annually—see below) can build up to look like mortar rendering[105] [Pl. 30].

Whitewashing with lime
Although the whitewashed cottage is the image on the Irish postcard, Gailey notes that widespread use of a 'whitewash' of lime became common only at a comparatively late date, at the end of the nineteenth century;[106] it may have started originally around the end of the eighteenth century, but not then for all cottages.[107] It seems that in the early days the limewash was considered to have cleansing and sterilising properties,[108] and indeed that in areas such as south Donegal as early as 1821 annual whitewashing was in vogue, 'seemingly having been introduced as a hygiene measure to combat outbreaks of typhus'.[109] More importantly, however, such limewash enhances the appearance of the vernacular

Pl. 21—The presence of a cluster of trees (usually sycamore) is a tell-tale sign of the site of an old Donegal cottage.

Pl. 22a—A cottage near Port which unusually is in an exposed position overlooking both lake and sea.

Pl. 22b—A now-demolished cottage at Horn Head which was exposed to coastal gales.

structures and looks just right in the Donegal countryside, being applied not only on the cottage walls but also (in the study area) on the gable projections (on each side of the roof), the chimney-stacks and the roof ridges, producing a 'boxed-in' effect[110] [Pl. 2b]. Additional whitewashing of the walls of outhouses and of field walls and gate-pillars enhances this scenic effect. Furthermore, the successive coats of limewash—usually applied each year and often by the woman of the house, as was the custom[111]—provide a sort of rendering like mortar on the stonework and enhance the undulating smooth appearance of walls[112] [Pls 29–30] while at the same time allowing moisture to evaporate.[113] As Gailey says, the traditional limewashed house was 'enlivened by subtle variation of surface created by successive layers of limewash applied direct to uneven stonework or even to plaster that softened but did not hide surface variations of the underlying material'.[114] For this latter reason misguided attempts to modernise such old cottages with a cement rendering can never create the same soft 'ripple' effect on the old, semi-projecting, underlying stone [Pls 10a, 31].

The gable ends

As already seen, the gable ends could change position as the 'longhouse' was added to over time, so that original gables carrying chimney-stacks could end up in the middle of the linear construction. Traditionally, end walls were unbroken by apertures at ground-floor level and so such walls in Donegal cottages are generally windowless and doorless,[115] it supposedly being unlucky to break such structures into an end gable.

Stepped stones are a particular feature of the tops of older gables.[116] In north Donegal slates laid on the flat were ideally suited to this purpose, held together by some mortar [Pl. 32]. Later, though, in the 1940s and '50s, it seems to have become common to add cemented projections formed in wooden moulds—locally called 'wind skews'—to the top of both gable ends, with a slight gable overhang to throw off the rain. These were then painted with whitewash to give a delightful boxed-in appearance to the roof. The reason for such constructions was not aesthetic but practical: the outer edges of the slates of Donegal cottages were prone to wind-lifting. The weight of the wind skews prevented this and also, by their slight prominence, raised the wind height, so giving some protection to the rest of the roof.

Sometimes the latter cemented feature is also to be found on interior 'gables' where the roof line changes [Pl. 33], thus further emphasising the

Pl. 23a—A typical Donegal 'boreen', flanked by stone walls, leading directly to an isolated cottage, now in ruins: such boreens are another clue to the site of old cottages.

Pl. 23b—A typical Donegal rounded gatepost (often whitewashed like the cottage to which it belonged).

Pl. 24—A threshing barn above a ruined cottage where once a horse would (from the outside foreground) have driven the machinery in the barn.

sectional historical development of the 'longhouse' roof. One of the advantages of the upright gable (and purlin roof) was that it made adding rooms much simpler, compared to the older style of hipped roof.[117] However, several examples of end gables in the study area now show signs of misalignment owing to lack of proper mortaring of stones [Pl. 34].

Roofs and roof timbers

Slates
One of the features of the linear dwelling was that it had a so-called 'gabled-type' roof with grey slates[118] since at least the nineteenth century, whereas thatched cottages tended to have hipped roofs, i.e. roofs sloping downwards at the gables to help throw off the wind.[119]

It appears that slating on farmhouse roofs may have progressed westwards from the east of Ireland as the nineteenth century progressed[120] and as stone quarries opened up.[121] Where slate was locally available, such materials of slate or thin flagstone—in somewhat irregular shapes and sizes[122] and often of different colour and texture from the stone walls[123]—made a more durable roof than thatch.

In the Dunfanaghy region the rough slates used were the so-called 'Roshine' slates, named after the quarries at Roshine where they were mined and which still exist [Pl. 35a].[124] It appears that the slate used for roofing was lifted from the top layer in such local quarries, whilst the deeper slate was thicker and was used as flags for floors. The authors learned from several older inhabitants in the area that their cottages were originally thatched but that the thatch was later replaced—on the main roofs at least—by the locally sourced slates, which would have been collected in relays by horse and cart direct from the quarries. Once the slates are properly laid, such roofs are very sound and as good as can be found anywhere, provided that the timbers underneath are strong enough to support them. The experience of one of the authors in respect of his own cottage roof is that, once on, they do not split and crack as may the non-indigenous 'Bangor blues' (the latter being apparently regarded by locals in more recent times as superior to the 'Roshines').

Being on the thick and slaty side, Roshine slates do form a heavy covering, and unfortunately in times past the supporting laths used were too thin for the job. Moreover, non-galvanised nails (which eventually rust) or even simple wooden pegs (which in time will bend and fail to

Pl. 25—An archive shot (c.1940s) of a cottage in Roshine with an elevated hayloft (and steps up) on the right-hand side; and, inset, how the same cottage looks today.

Pl. 26a—Typical local vernacular dry-stone cottage construction, with larger stones used on the corners.

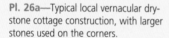

Pl. 26b—An example of old building economy? Here a large boulder at ground level has been crudely incorporated (still in its original position) as part of the cottage back wall!

hold) were used to secure the slates onto the laths. The result has been that over time many such roofs have suffered severe slate slippage when the laths break or give way and/or the nails or pegs fail [Pl. 35b].

The Roshine slates did not always split to a regular size so that their thickness can vary from slate to slate, and they are difficult to shape to a completely rectangular form without splitting. However, these very features add to their rustic and aesthetic charm, as do their variant hues, their surface often being streaked with ironstone staining, giving a grey and ochreish effect [Pl. 36]. The attractive appearance of the roof is further enhanced by the method of laying the slate rows—large ones at the bottom of the roof, with the slate lengths progressively diminishing towards the crown [e.g. Pl. 33]. This is yet another example of vernacular continuity, here caused by old roof patterns being faithfully followed by local builders.[125] Sometimes 'flag-size' slates were used in the study area to roof outhouses; in these cases the rough and irregular overlap of the slates gives a very rustic appearance, as in one Roshine farmstead [Pl. 37].

A further—and possibly later—enhancement of the roof has been the practice of applying mortar or cement around the edges of individual slates to limit wind and rain penetration. This gives a charming light and dark grey aspect to the whole roof. In some cases lime plaster might also have been applied to the underside of the slates to prevent wind penetration through the cracks and to eliminate any drips of condensation falling below in damp weather.

When the slates were laid, marked sticks were used to grade the various lengths [Pl. 38], and a metal tool with a sharp point on the bent end was used to peck a hole in each individual slate through which the nail or wooden peg would be inserted.

Unfortunately, in more recent times, as seen above, Roshine slates have been stripped from old roofs and replaced by asbetos-type slates, which lack the same vernacular character [e.g. Pls 10a, 11a] and indeed in some cases have started deteriorating badly [Pl. 39]. In other cases such modern slates have been combined with others of a more vernacular character [Pl. 40].

Thatch and other materials
Though it seems difficult to imagine today,[126] many of the now grey-slated cottage roofs in the Dunfanaghy region would originally have been thatched, slate only being seen as a superior roofing material in later times. For example, in the Derryreel area it appears that some fifteen or so

Pl. 27a—(Left) A rare two-storey cottage at Horn Head with slate-lintelled windows.

Pl. 27b—(Above) Another example of slate being used (instead of wood) above windows as lintels, and below as sills.

Pl. 28—Unmortared drystone walling is also locally common (here of local Roshine slates).

Pl. 29—The typical external appearance of walls where lime plaster or limewash has been used, giving a natural rippled effect.

of the old cottages were originally thatched and were slated later [Pl. 41]. The nature of the rounded roof gables[127] of some ruins in the Dunfanaghy region indicates that these cottages remained thatched until their abandonment [Pl. 42a–d]. The thatching was usually carried out with the local sea grass called 'bent'. This was obtained from the coastal sand-dunes, where it was cut with a hook. The grass is very tough, and cutting it under the sand was thought to be the easiest way to harvest it—though with the result, especially at Horn Head, that the dunes needed to be replanted to stop sand blowing in the wind. It was good material and could last for up to four years before re-thatching was needed. Further inland—particularly around Creeslough and towards Glenveigh—it appears that, owing to its ready availability,[128] an inferior material was used: this was a coarse mountain (and bogland) grass, reputedly called *deabh* in the local dialect.[129] However, this material had a short lifespan and was often used only for outbuildings. Even more inferior as a thatching material was the rush—seemingly, like *deabh*, used mostly on farm outbuildings, where it had to be renewed each year owing to rotting [Pl. 43].

Overlapping layers of sods or 'scraws' were invariably used as an underthatch [Pl. 44] (usually with the vegetation side uppermost), even where not necessary to anchor thatching-pins ('scollops' of hazel or bramble)[130] [Pl. 45]. Usually these scraws were supported underneath by thin strips of split bog timber or flat branches[131] [Pl. 44]. The scraws essentially provided an insulating base for the outer thatching. On top of this thatching a network of ropes would have been applied, in criss-cross fashion,[132] as a protection against wind damage, though not in inland locations [Pl. 46]. Normally these would have been ropes of plaited oat straw,[133] originally home-made, fashioned with a special twisting-hook[134]—known locally as the 'trahook'—that was made from bent wire in the shape of a car starting-handle. The method was for the man of the house—usually sitting on a stool at the barn door—to get one of his children to put the hook in a length of straw and to keep twisting whilst backing down the 'street', while he fed the straw into the developing rope. When a length was twisted it was rolled into a ball called a 'clew', and the process was repeated until there was enough rope for the thatching. Such ropes had a short life—often less than a year on a roof—but they were also used for the thatching of corn stacks [Pl. 47] and the weaving of neck collars for horses. Later on it appears that imported Indian grass rope, bought from local stores, came to be used for these

Pl. 30—A well-maintained cottage in the Kildarragh area where the fresh paint on the external walls enhances the ripple effect of the stonework.

Pl. 31—An old cottage where the walls have been stripped of lime plaster and now appear to be cement-rendered.

Pl. 32—A good example of the use of stepped slates as gable ends.

Pl. 33—A still-lived-in cottage in Dunfanaghy with typical whitewashed roof ridges and wind skews.

sorts of purposes.

Typical of the Dunfanaghy region is the use of stone pegs—sometimes in crude shapes—set into the stonework under the eaves to hold down the latitudinal thatching ropes[135] [Pl. 48], with similar pegs (but often wooden) taking the longitudinal ropes at the gables [Pl. 49]. It would appear that, like other vernacular building practices, thatching would have been carried out without the use of sophisticated tools, on a 'cooperative neighbourly basis',[136] with family and possibly also neighbours being involved.

As can be seen from the few remaining old cottages in the Dunfanaghy area, roofing materials often differed in the various sections of the 'longhouse' roof line. On outbuildings in later times the 'tin' (corrugated iron) came to be much favoured. This, when painted in the traditional red or green oxide paint, still fits in well with the traditional vernacular aspect[137] [Pl. 50a–b], though not when left unpainted [Pl. 50c].

The roof ridge and wallplate

As has been seen, the traditional Donegal 'longhouse' often started life as a single unit which was then added to in a linear fashion on one or both sides. Today the 'joins' can be seen at wall level, and the stepped roof heights of the added units can also vary to a greater or lesser degree,[138] with often a small rounded 'bump' where the internal dividing wall comes up, or even a sag [Pl. 51]: this can give some further external indication of the number of internal 'units' or rooms. In particular, the roof lines of byre sections usually drop[139] [e.g. Pls 14a, 15c], though not always. A feature of many 'longhouses' in the Dunfanaghy region is the addition at the end of a two-storey hayloft, which breaks the continuity of an otherwise single-storey dwelling. The unified appearance of such a structure is enhanced by the fact that it is roofed in the same slates as the rest of the dwelling. Access to the loft was traditionally by means of stone steps leading up at the front of the cottage, which adds further character to the unit [Pl. 52; see also Pl. 103b]. This unit was two-storey for a practical reason, for the back of the hayloft was sometimes built into a bank for convenience to give ground-level access for storing corn and hay [Pl. 52], and this made it easy for the farmer to feed his cattle in the byre below by dropping hay down to them.[140]

In more modern times at least, the roof ridge—where the roof ridge board is usually of thin construction—was often cemented in a continuous and rounded or angled line and then whitewashed; this,

Pl. 34—A typical example of a now-roofless small building (near Falcarragh) where the gable walls have started to angle out and the one remaining purlin is near to collapse.

Pl. 35a—A slate quarry in Roshine which is still worked, showing the former source of local slates and flags.

Pl. 35b—A (sadly) common sight—slippage of heavy Roshine slates, leading in time to rotting of timbers beneath.

combined with the gable 'wind skews' (see above), gave a 'boxed-in' effect to the whole roof, emphasising its rectangular shape.

The wallplate of the Donegal cottage is usually of wood, but sometimes a large slate, supporting the roof joists, is used instead in the Dunfanaghy region.[141]

The roof beams

A prevalent type of purlin in the slated cottage roof in the study area is of 'bog timber' or 'bog fir', i.e. those timbers found preserved in the peat bogs during the cutting of turf [Pl. 53a–b]. In the virtually treeless areas of north Donegal such 'fossil' timbers became an important roofing material as the eighteenth century progressed,[142] particularly in the poorer rural communities such as those under consideration,[143] where the landlord would in any case have usually owned what few big trees existed. Ordnance Survey memoirs in the 1830s contain frequent references to the use of bog wood for roofing.[144] Such timbers were typically used in the collar-beam truss form of roof (see below).

In addition to being used for major beams such as roof-trusses and purlins, such bog timber, when split, also commonly served as a base for the underthatch of scraws in thatched houses [Pls 43, 44].

The 'collar-beam' truss

Gailey states that, in districts close to north Donegal, trusses with raised blades were commonly 'crudely shaped' out of bog timber and other woods, giving rounded roof profiles usually associated with 'roped-thatched roofs'.[145] Amazingly, several examples of this type of roof still survive in some cottages in the Dunfanaghy region, but usually only in byres[146] [Pl. 54].

The essence of the collar-beam method of roof construction—which was a later development from the 'full cruck' type[147]—was that the trusses, most commonly lacking tie-beams at wall-head height, usually rested in a straight line from the wall heads,[148] being tied at the upper end by one or two 'collar-beams' or braces (i.e. short cross-pieces, sometimes including an additional lower brace or 'reliever'); so that, unlike conventional beams meeting at the apex (see below),[149] the upper collar 'scarfs' (i.e. joins endwise) the two trusses,[150] producing a rounded roof profile suitable for thatching by smoothing the angle of the ridge.[151] These transverse collar-beams—apparently called 'couple-hooves'[152] in County Donegal—were pegged to the trusses with wooden pegs and set in halved

Pl. 36—The local Roshine slates are usually grey but are flecked with yellowish iron-stone, so giving a pleasant overall mottled effect to the roof.

Pl. 37—The outhouse of a Roshine cottage which is crudely slated with large overlapping flagstones.

Pl. 38—Use of an original notched stick—with graded measurements—here being held against a Roshine slate to gauge its size for roofing purposes.

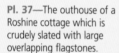

notched joints[153] [Pl. 54]. Such principal rafter trusses thus helped to carry the roof and to support it at a distance from the end gables.[154]

The conventional purlin system

The more usual (and generally later[155]) roof-beam system in Donegal cottages was that of 'longitudinal heavy purlins with their ends bedded in gables and internal partition wall' without any interposing transverse beams[156] [see Pl. 53b]. In the Dunfanaghy region the characteristics of the local bog fir dictated that these did not usually extend to more than 15ft spans, making (as seen) the average room length between 12ft and 15ft. The mass walls—the gables and internal transverse walls rising to the apex—could then take the weight via the purlins. Thus it was found that 'internal partition walls could suitably replace [the old roof truss system] altogether'.[157] In the typical 'three-purlin'-length cottage of the Dunfanaghy area, two such purlins—usually of bog fir but sometimes of massive sawn wood (some of it perhaps scavenged as driftwood from the Donegal shoreline[158])—carried much of the weight of the roof. The scarcity of timber favoured this type of construction because it minimised the number of heavy timbers needed to roof a house.[159] With few heavy timbers, closely spaced rafter timbers generally overlapped the usually solitary and massive purlins across each roof side—from wall head up to the ridge board—making a roof strong enough to carry heavy slates such as those from the Roshine quarries.

On top of the rafters was nailed appropriately spaced horizontal lathing for hanging slates;[160] unfortunately in the study area this lathing was often not thick enough to bear the weight of the local slates (hence the prevalent 'slippage' and fall damage). The slates were affixed by one nail or wooden peg to the laths in rows of diminishing slate lengths (typical also of roofing in other parts of Ireland) towards the crown of the roof[161] [see e.g. Pl. 35b].

Chimneys

In Irish cottages, the placing of chimneys on the roof line, 'reflecting axially located hearths', has been seen as one of the characteristics of such dwellings.[162] Although the gable-sited chimney was the norm,[163] if additional rooms were later added lengthways such cottages became so-called 'central-hearth houses'.[164] Thus many surviving examples of cottages in the Dunfanaghy region, built initially as one- or two-unit structures, now have two chimneys (in addition to any possible added

41

Pl. 39—An isolated cottage, at some time re-roofed with poor asbestos slates which have started to curl.

Pl. 40—A roof line at Horn Head which is composed of several types of materials in individual sections, including old slates and newer ones.

Pl. 41—One of the remaining inhabited cottages in Derryreel, where the main roof still has the old slates, but which would originally have been thatched.

gable chimneys) breaking the central portions of the roof line. Typically, the large square top of the stone-built and lime-plastered stack is flat on top, without any form of pot—a feature which unfortunately allows rain to enter onto the fire below. On the upper part of the stack a line of slates was typically built in to make a protruding lip to throw off the rain [e.g. Pls 2a, 41], whilst the bottom of the stack was given a fillet of plaster or cement around the junction with the slates to form a crude sort of waterproof flashing (prone to cracking—and subsequent water leakage—in cold weather).

Other external features

The 'outshot' (cailleach)

It seems that this feature—which can be seen externally as a rectangular protrusion usually on the back wall and as a continuation outwards of the main roof extending in a straight line[165]—is typical of most (but not all) of the surviving cottages in the Dunfanaghy region. It was characteristic of north-western districts of Ireland,[166] becoming traditional in the vernacular Irish building style in later centuries, so that, for example, it was used to provide an additional sleeping unit in byre-dwellings from the nineteenth century onwards. Internally, the outshot accommodated a bed in a corner of the living accommodation, i.e. the kitchen, close to the hearth to take advantage of the heat of the fire.[167] It was here that, traditionally, the senior occupants of the dwelling slept.[168] It is usually to be found on the side wall nearest to the chimney end of a dwelling[169] for reasons of cosiness [Pl. 55a], so that in the Dunfanaghy area outshots are invariably to be found at the rear wall of the cottage on the opposite side to the door [Pl. 55a–c]. This nook in the wall gave a narrow room extra width—and a consequent saving of space—where most needed by the fire, especially in times when sizeable rafter timbers were not easy to obtain to construct broad rooms,[170] though Gailey does not consider that such features constitute a 'late expedient introduced to overcome overcrowding'.[171]

As the outshot has usually to be big enough to take a double bed, in its more extensive examples the internal projection can be up to 80cm deep [Pl. 55a].[172] However, some examples of outshots in the Dunfanaghy region are much shallower (in at least one case only about 6in. deep), making one wonder whether they housed furniture other than beds[173] [Pl. 56]. It seems, in fact, that outshots in the northern area of their distribution

Pl. 42a—A now-roofless three-room cottage ruin, which may have been thatched.

Pl. 42b—The remains of another cottage that would have been thatched.

Pl. 42c—The last remains of thatch on the same cottage.

Pl. 42d—A building with rounded gables, indicating that it was once thatched.

in Ireland are generally shallower than elsewhere; so that in such cases much of the bed protruded into the kitchen floor area.[174] On the other hand, in one cottage in the study area the top room has in effect a 'double' outshot that takes up the whole of that part of the back wall (18ft long) and extends out to a depth of some 51in., forming two extra bedrooms under the same roof projection and partitioned off into two alcoves by thin stone walls (now demolished) [Pls 57, 70]. Because of such variability of size, even in the same district, Gailey is of the opinion that the outshot should 'not be regarded as sufficient basis to define a house type'. The length of the outshot is, however, fairly standard at about 6ft internally, being as 'long only as the bed it accommodated'.[175]

The bed contained in the outshot often took the form of a settle bed, i.e. 'a bench-seat with a fairly high back [or sides] by day', or of a hinged construction opening out to make up a low bed if required at night[176] (the 'bench' seat could be opened for the storage of a mattress or blankets). The 'bed' was often screened off from the rest of the kitchen by day by means of a curtain, or even timber doors.[177] (As will be seen, in surviving inhabited cottages in the Dunfanaghy region curtains are still used in living areas such as kitchens to give privacy to beds in a corner of a room without an outshot [Pls 71, 72].) In its older form, the wall-bed could have had a bog-timber frame and a mattress made of wattles or ropes twisted from root fibres of bog fir, and may even have had its own canopy or 'tester' overhead.[178] Generally, no windows were broken into the outshot.[179]

The porch
A small porch around the front door is typical of cottages in the Dunfanaghy area, all such protrusions having a small flat roof of their own (as compared to the sloping 'shared' main roof in the case of the outshot[180]). These may have been added as features in the late nineteenth century.[181] This porch was generally roofed with large, thick local slates [Pl. 58a–d] laid on top of each other. Such features were shallowly built,[182] extending out not usually more than 2ft from the otherwise straight main walls (about 3ft 6in. to 4ft from the inside front wall), thus forming a sort of mini-room in which the externally hinged main door (and any additional half-door) could swing. The typical Donegal cottage had no closed-off lobby inside the front walls, being of a 'direct-entry' pattern.[183] The side piers of the porch—which abut the side frames of the front door—are typically about 1ft 6in. thick and of mass stone construction,[184]

Pl. 43—Re-thatching of a cottage byre in Roshine with newly cut rushes, the greenness of which soon turns to light brown.

Pl. 44—Existing underthatch in a local cottage roof where fir branches have been used as a base.

Pl. 45—One of the few remaining re-thatched cottages in north Donegal (at Ballinadrait) showing scalloping.

Pl. 46—A more complete view of the same cottage.

the outer side limits being typically some 6ft to 6ft 6in. wide. The height is usually just slightly more than the height of the door itself, i.e. about 6ft 6in. from the ground. The main purpose of such porches was no doubt to act as windbreaks around doors,[185] though they have a limited effect in protecting door bottoms from rotting in the absence of any guttering. It appears that the flat roofs were also popular places to put the baked bread to cool, away from the possible predations of chickens or children! Extending outside around the outer base of the porch is often to be found a small rectangle of flags leading to the raised doorstep [Pl. 59a].

In the case of some surviving Donegal cottages disproportionately large porches have been added in more recent times, with an extra door on the side [e.g. Pls 33, 51, 59b, 62].

Stone bench
A pleasing minor feature of cottages in the Dunfanaghy region is the small stone bench set against the front wall, usually to the right of the entrance. Invariably the top is formed of a single large rectangular slate 'flag' supported on two stone plinths [Pl. 60]. Besides the obvious purpose of providing an occasional outside seat for members of the household [Pl. 61], and sometimes for passing travellers, such benches had several uses. The bench often held a bucket of spring water flanked by a 'pandie' (a tin container made by tinkers) from which travellers or members of the household could drink; it also formed a convenient base for the washing of clothes in a tin bath. It was used for drying pots and pans[186] and as a place for the man of the house to wash and shave in the morning [Pl. 62]. As cottages in former times had no mains water supply, all household water had to be drawn from a nearby spring, which was usually the women's task; and where a yoke and buckets system was used, the bench provided a handy place for resting full buckets of water.

Doors

The main door
The Irish cottage traditionally has wooden match-boarded doors with lapped joints—sometimes consisting of broad boards 'false-beaded' to suggest narrower ones and usually (from the second half of the nineteenth century at any rate) having bevelled edges, secured at the back with three transverse battens.[187] Typically they would have been about 6ft

Pl. 47—An unusual sight in County Donegal today— a thatched corn stack, complete with plaited straw ropework.

Pl. 48—Projecting stone pegs under the eaves of an outhouse roof in Roshine, to which would have been attached ropes for holding down the thatch.

Pl. 49—Projecting stone (and wooden) pegs were also used, as here, along the gable eaves to take the longitudinal ropes.

high and 3ft broad, surmounted by a slate (or stone) lintel, though in some small cottages with low outer walls the doors are no more than 5ft high [Pls 63, 64; see also Pl. 74], implying that even small inhabitants might have had to stoop to enter! A practical reason for such low doorways may have been the need to economise on stone in the construction of the walls and to get the roof on as soon as possible.

The external door opened directly into the kitchen (or the entrance from porch to kitchen)[188] in the typical 'direct-entry cottage' (i.e. one having no internal lobby). Gailey makes great play of the fact that the front door in Irish rural houses almost always led directly into the unit used as the principal living space or kitchen, and in fact it was often positioned off-centre to reflect the position of the kitchen.[189]

Some Donegal cottages appear to have had opposite doors so that one could be shut whilst the other was kept open away from the wind.[190] Estyn Evans, for example, says that a 'very general feature' throughout the north and west of Ireland was the 'presence of two doors in the kitchen, one opposite the other'.[191] However, all the cottages that the writers have seen in the Dunfanaghy region appear only to have one or more doors on the front, the back of the cottage being in any case often set into a bank, making rear access impossible. Like windows in the Dunfanaghy region, doors were typically topped by a large slate lintel [Pl. 64].

The 'half-door'
This has long been a supposed feature of the vernacular Irish dwelling, but it appears to be wrong to regard it as 'peculiarly Irish'[192] or, indeed, even as a particular hallmark of Donegal cottages. As Gailey comments:[193] 'It is paradoxical that an element most popularly associated with traditional rural Irish houses is undocumented: the half door. By no means all farmhouses and cottages were provided with one, but they occurred in all districts, mostly amongst smaller farmers and landless folk.' Thus the half-door is probably a nineteenth-century feature which may have been inspired by the bottom halves of horizontally divided stable doors. It was, when fitted, a feature of the front entrance, and was hinged outside a full-length door so that both opened neatly inwards.

In the Dunfanaghy region half-doors were usually hung on two pintles attached to the main door frame, but in the case of surviving cottages no original examples seem now to exist *in situ* [Pl. 65].

Undoubtedly, the main purpose of the half-door was to let extra light into cottages with only small windows while keeping free-ranging farm

Pl. 50a—An old cottage now completely roofed in tin—but still retaining its vernacular look—seemingly now used as a holiday home.

Pl. 50b—A range of tin roofs on some buildings on Horn Head.

Pl. 50c—A derelict cottage where the tin roof section is rusting badly. Note the unusual style of asbestos slates used on the main part of the roof.

Pl. 51—One of the most picturesque remaining cottages still lived in, which has a charming dip in one section of the roof line.

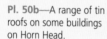

animals such as hens out of the kitchen. As has been aptly stated,[194] 'Perhaps the popularity of the half-door first related to the expense of providing glazed windows in poorer homes, where it remained a barrier of the full door so far as wandering animals of the farmyard were concerned, yet it admitted light'. It was important, too, in controlling draught to the turf-burning open hearth,[195] and from a social standpoint it was also 'a convenient arm-rest' for contemplation or conversation with a passing neighbour.[196]

Windows

The windows of cottages in the study area are undoubtedly some of the most charming vernacular features, albeit borrowed from the loftier and more formal Georgian-style tradition,[197] being traditionally brightly painted (together sometimes with the sills and surrounds [Pl. 66])—in the Dunfanaghy area invariably in the stock 'cottage' colours of red, green or blue, providing a vivid contrast to the otherwise whitewashed walls.[198]

Such windows were usually few and small—in the Dunfanaghy region on average about 3ft 6in. high and 2ft wide[199] [Pl. 67a–f]. Traditionally Irish cottage windows were placed by preference on the side away from the prevailing winds, even if this meant missing out on available sea views! In the study area windows are to be found not only on the front walls[200] but also on the back, where they tend to be smaller[201] [Pl. 67e]. Their lintels are formed by large slates (often also used as sills) [Pl. 67f]. The positioning of such windows depended very much on the internal layout of rooms, at least one window being allocated per room.[202]

The remaining older windows in the study area are of the sliding sash variety[203] with 'ears' to the sashes, a style which may have become popular in the early nineteenth century[204] and apparently replaced earlier versions.[205] Exceptionally in the study area those cottages with sleeping-lofts in the roof could have a small gable window high up or even right under the side roof eaves[206] [Pl. 68a–b]. Each sash typically has a single or double row of two to three rectangular Georgian-style panes set in crossing glazing bars.[207] The insides of window opes in the study area are often chamfered outwards so as to widen the opening [Pls 27a, 67d] in order to admit more light.[208] Blocked-up windows—particularly in present-day byres adjacent to dwelling sections—may of course suggest earlier human habitation in such sections.[209]

Pl. 52—(Left) An old cottage in Roshine with a substantial two-storey 'half-loft' section to the right, accessed by stone steps in the front.

Pl. 53a—(Below left) A derelict roof still supported by the original bog timbers.

Pl. 53b—(Below right) Rough timbers still supporting an old roof of Roshine slates.

Pl. 54—A rare surviving example of a roof truss made of bog timber in the outhouse of a cottage in Roshine.

INTERNAL FEATURES

Layout and size of rooms

In the typical cottage in the study area—the 'three-purlin' cottage—the central room would be the kitchen, with doorways (connecting inner doors made, like the front door, of sheeted timber, ledged and braced[210]) through the internal mass walls (and on the same side) to access the 'upper' and 'lower' rooms, which were generally bedrooms of similar or smaller size,[211] often with a step up in the floor level from the living-room. In addition to the mass dividing walls extending up to the roof apex, internal partitions, usually of wooden stud [Pl. 69] but sometimes of stone [Pl. 70], were added to subdivide direct-entry houses, particularly on the back wall of the kitchen[212] and bedrooms.[213] Such 'stud-and-board' partitions internally divided a longhouse into units—often with a gap between the top of the partition and the ceiling—and were erected at a later period,[214] so that what was originally a single room could become up to three rooms within the same floor area, providing extra sleeping areas in overcrowded cottages.[215] Gailey refers to an 'increased emphasis on personal privacy' in the later nineteenth century,[216] and it appears that such partitioning was put in place particularly to give the female offspring of the house some privacy.[217]

More provisional 'partitioning' is also to be found in the Dunfanaghy region, where—even if no outshot exists—at least one example remains of the use of the kitchen dresser, set at right angles to the kitchen wall, to form one 'wall' of a sleeping alcove, the other side being closed off with a curtain running on a string from the dresser top to the back wall[218] [Pl. 71]; and there are still examples in the region of beds in kitchens being curtained off in a corner to give some sort of privacy [Pl. 72].

Ceilings

Unceilinged roofs were common in Irish vernacular houses until late in the nineteenth century[219] [Pl. 73]; until recently at least one example still existed at Horn Head, where the underside of the roof open to the rafters was blackened by years of turf smoke [Pl. 74]. However, from the nineteenth century tongue-and-groove timber sheeting—mostly at wall-head height—began to feature in Irish cottages[220] [see e.g. Pls 69, 75],

Pl. 55a—A typical Donegal 'outshot' next to the fire. Note that its ceiling is separately lined with matching board to make it cosier.

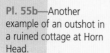

Pl. 55b—Another example of an outshot in a ruined cottage at Horn Head.

Pl. 55c—A slated outshot behind a cottage in Roshine. Note that the roof line to the extremity of the outshot is continuous and keeps to the angle of the main roof as part of the integral cottage construction.

perhaps as a symbol of modernity and no doubt with the practical purpose of helping to conserve heat and to exclude draughts coming from ill-fitting roof slates.[221] In any event, this type of ceiling, often dark-painted, is now commonly to be seen in the living-rooms of surviving cottages in the Dunfanaghy area.

The 'half-loft'

Sleeping-lofts in one end of the roof, often lit by a small gable window,[222] were quite common in Irish cottages[223] to provide extra accommodation for overcrowded families;[224] they usually contained one or two beds and were used by the boys of the family. They took various forms but were always accessed by a ladder, and in some cases a bedroom was even constructed over an adjacent byre as a lofted sleeping-chamber lit by a small, high gable window.[225] A section of the roof space nearest the gable end[226] could be partitioned off as a vertically triangular space for sleeping, with flooring added at wallplate height;[227] but many such spaces were left open, which meant that it was common for children who slept there to lie listening to any tales that might be told around the fire below. Such lofts could occupy up to a third of the kitchen roof space and in some cases the roof height could be raised in this area. If partitioned, access to such lofts would be by a small door above the ladder. In the area of study few examples exist, and one at least has no gable window, so that it had no natural light [Pl. 75].

The kitchen

As seen, the kitchen formed the heart of a Donegal cottage, often occupying a central position after later additions of bedrooms or byres on either side of it. Large and usually rectangular in shape, the Irish kitchen was for a long time the social centre of family life[228] and was provided for this purpose with furniture placed around its sides.[229] As also seen, kitchens were regularly used as sleeping places,[230] whether in the outshot or in an area curtained off for privacy. Warm though the kitchen was for sleeping in, there was a consequential problem—crickets. These insects in times past inhabited almost every rural Donegal house, living in the stone wall around the fire, where they relished the heat. At night, when the

Pl. 56—A very shallow outshot (to left) in a ruined cottage in Roshine. The bank visible through the window rises almost from the level of the window-sill.

Pl. 57—A rare example of a large 'double' outshot with two windows inserted, allowing two additional bedrooms to be partitioned off inside.

lights were put out, the crickets would come out and jump about the floor, singing and chirping noisily (especially if rain was on the way). Where the settle-bed was at ground level, an additional problem arose: the crickets might hop onto the bed, causing further sleeplessness as well as, for good measure, feasting on the woollen bankets and riddling them with holes!

Some cottages in the study area appear to possess a small pantry as a separate room adjacent to the kitchen [Pl. 76].

The hearth and fire
The hearth in the Irish cottage was the 'very core of the house'[231] and the social centre around which any entertaining was normally done.[232] Within it, the turf fire was indeed the heart of the home and was never allowed to burn out, being rekindled each morning.[233] Each night the man or woman of the house would 'rake' the fire at bedtime, a ritual which was carefully carried out. The burning embers would be pulled back with the tongs and a row of damp turf, taken from the outside of the stack, placed at the back and on the hearth. All the burning embers were then piled up on top of the turf, and the ashes were shovelled on top of these to slow combustion overnight. In the morning the burning embers would be raked out with the tongs, the ashes pulled to one side and disposed of in the ash bucket. When fresh dry turf was applied to the embers, the fire would quickly come to life.

In later times, and with the advent of chimney flues, the hearth was set against a gable, and usually against the wall at the opposite end of the kitchen to the 'direct-entry' door.[234] Typically a smoke channel was constructed into the face of the 'hearth wall itself' in the case of the stone-built cottages of Donegal in the nineteenth century.[235] Thus the extruding 'breastwork' type of flue (rare in surviving Dunfanaghy area cottages) [Pl. 77] became outmoded and the flue came to be completely contained within the wall thickness.[236]

In the Dunfanaghy area, a particular vernacular feature was the use as a lintel[237] and flue formers above the fire of two or more 1in.-thick slates (flags), 1ft or more in height and edge-on to each other in ascending height (not always in a completely straight line), running up to, or near to, the roof apex [Pl. 78a–c]—for example, a construction of three end-on slates, varying from 1ft to just over 2ft high. The bottom slate was usually canted out slightly (but only about 3in.) to form a very slight chimney-breast, resting on corbels formed of a largish cantilevered protruding topstone, supported by stepped small stones beneath [Pl. 79]. The

Pl. 58a—An old cottage with a symmetrically placed central porch.

Pl. 58b—Here the porch has a very narrow projection from the front wall.

Pl. 58c—An abandoned cottage with vegetation now growing on the flat porch roof.

Pl. 58d—An 'off-centre' example of a traditional north Donegal porch.

chimney flue gradually narrowed as it proceeded upwards. It appears that these 'flue' flags—now often exposed to the elements in ruined examples—were originally lime-plastered to merge with the rest of the stone gable [see Pl. 78a]. In at least one two-storey vernacular cottage in the Dunfanaghy region, the main chimney has a channel branching off at first-floor level to accommodate a bedroom fire [Pl. 80]. Sometimes the only fire lintel is a crude long stone [Pl. 81a–b] or infilled stonework [Pl. 82].

The fire itself was usually positioned at ground level, on a stone slab (as in the above-mentioned cottage at Horn Head [see Pl. 6a]) or built on a small mound of oval stones collected from the beach, and was surrounded by stone flags[238] which might crack if immediately under the fire. The fire was sometimes flanked by simple hobs built into the gable stonework [see Pl. 77] (as in the case of the reconstructed Donegal cottage at Cultra); in larger hearths, fireside seats might be incorporated—the left-hand one sometimes being 'hers' and the right-hand one 'his'.[239] In the Dunfanaghy area, however, the hearths are usually small, about 2–3ft high and about 3ft wide [Pl. 82]. In later times the fire position was often raised because provision of a forced draught for coal-burning required a raised grate—a feature that was not necessary for turf, which demanded slow burning[240] [Pl. 83]. Many surviving Donegal cottages now have raised grates fronted by metal bars [see e.g. Pl. 77]. Metal ranges and built-in ovens were also a later feature of Donegal cottages[241] [Pl. 84], a feature which sadly led over time to the removal and loss of the old original fireside cranes.

The second half of the nineteenth century saw an expansion of the fireplace to heat other cottage rooms, with separate flues also serving bedrooms,[242] where the fireplaces (though similar in construction) tended to be smaller than those in the kitchen and, in the Dunfanaghy region, were usually surrounded by brightly painted wooden mantelpieces of simple design [Pl. 85a–b]. As a result, most of the multi-chimneyed house sections there are in reality of a later vintage[243] owing to the piecemeal extension of an originally smaller central gable-chimneyed unit by bedrooms with individual fireplaces [see e.g. Pl. 2b].

The crane

A black metal crane—usually locally made by the blacksmith[244]—was traditional in the Irish kitchen fireplace [Pl. 86a–b]. This device was designed to have a swivel top and bottom to swing over the open fire; the

Pl. 59a—(Above left) The porch of a former cottage at Horn Head, surrounded (typically) by an area of paved flagstones.

Pl. 59b—(Above) A more modern example of a cottage porch in the region, complete with its own windows.

Pl. 60—(Left) A typical north Donegal stone seat adjacent to the porch.

process was facilitated by the traditional position of the fire at floor level.[245] On the top bar of the crane hung—and swung—the kettle [Pl. 87b] and cooking pots attached to a 'pot-hanger' (or hangers) hooked onto it, by means of which the height of the hanging utensil could be easily adjusted[246] [Pl. 87a]. A lot of boiling was done in a large pot [Pl. 87b] which the woman of the house had to handle, for both cooking and laundry purposes. For cooking, the empty pot was hung on the pot-hanger before the contents and water were added. After cooking potatoes, the pot had to be carefully swung off the fire and the boiling water had to be emptied out, a process known as 'teaming the spuds'. It was effected by catching the leg of the pot with a cloth hanging by the fireside. The pot was tilted with the lid slightly off, and the boiling water was drained into a bucket sitting underneath. The pot was then briefly swung back over the fire to dry the potatoes, and as many as were needed for the meal were then lifted out. Any left over were later 'pounded' with a wooden pounder as hen or pig feed.

The crane could also be used for drying smaller items of laundry such as socks. Unfortunately, as these would be made of wool, the crickets around the fire would come out at night and feast on them, peppering them with holes more efficiently than any moth!

Usually the crane was positioned to the left of the hearth, which was more convenient for a right-handed wife, though Estyn Evans points out that such left-hand siting also follows the direction of the sun's movement in the sky.[247] Strangely, several of the remaining cranes still *in situ* in cottages in the Dunfanaghy region are positioned to the right[248] [see e.g. Pl. 86a–b], indicating, perhaps, a number of left-handed women in the area in the past! The typical height of these cranes is some 3ft, the height being of course dictated by the height of the fire lintel into, and beneath which, it had to swing.

An alternative arrangement was to hang pots from a chain around a so-called 'rantle-tree'—a metal bar set across the chimney cavity.[249] This feature, as in an existing cottage in Drimnaraw [Pl. 77], could be some distance up the chimney. Although all such features were made obsolete by the introduction of ranges and fixed stoves,[250] a surprising number of old cranes still exist even in the ruined cottages of the Dunfanaghy region.

'Keeping holes'

Many of the cottages in the Dunfanaghy area have these small alcoves on one or both sides of the fire. They are about 2ft high by 1ft broad,

Pl. 61—Former inhabitants of a cottage in Roshine (together with two children of one of the authors) gathered around an old stone seat.

Pl. 62—An example of a stone bench by a modernised porch on which washing utensils are still evident!

Pl. 63—A cottage with low lintels over the doors.

sometimes surrounded by a wooden edging [Pl. 87c–d]. Such keeping holes were used for storing knick-knacks such as pipes or even, in at least one case, for displaying an eight-day clock. It seems that traditionally, where there were two such holes, one was for the woman's possessions and the other for the man's. Such wall holes seem to have been traditional in Irish cottages generally.[251]

In the Dunfanaghy region there are also several examples of larger alcoves being set into the internal mass walls and fitted with shelves and/or cupboard doors [Pl. 88]. All such features—including boards of cup-hooks on walls [Pl. 89]—helped to make the best use of the limited space for storage of household items. A choice place for a wall press was near the fire so that the contents—typically salt, pepper and sugar—could be kept dry; the press might also house baking utensils and some of the best delph.

The dresser
The dresser was typical of Donegal cottage kitchens, as elsewhere in Ireland, where it was one of the most important pieces of furniture,[252] standing either against the kitchen side wall or, more commonly, against the partition between kitchen and bedroom opposite the fire[253] [Pl. 90a–b]. Typically the lower part comprised a closed cupboard with two hinged matchwood doors,[254] surmounted by a drawer holding cutlery, or—more crudely—simply a curtain held up with string. As for the upper part, on the broad top surface of the lower section delph bowls were 'whammeled' (set out as a pyramid), whilst further rows of delph were displayed on the shallower shelves above. North Donegal cottages typically had three top shelves where cups/mugs were arranged on hooks, and plates and bowls were typically set on end and held upright by rows of moulded wooden bars to the front[255] [see Pl. 90a]. Such dressers were regularly painted by the woman of the house in bright colours (e.g. a contrasting green and white).

As seen above, the dresser could have another useful purpose in the Donegal kitchen, namely that of forming an additional short partition wall for a bedroom by being turned round at 90% to the wall with a curtain hung from dresser to the main wall on a long pole or string [see e.g. Pl. 75].

Pl. 64—Another example of a door with a low lintel made of slate.

Pl. 65—A renovated cottage at Horn Head where the present 'half-door' appears to be of modern construction.

Pl. 66—A former cottage at Port where the old sash windows and surrounds were painted in one of the colours traditional locally (green, red and blue).

The table

This has been said to constitute the third most significant piece of furniture in the kitchen,[256] and in Donegal cottages a pine table seems typically to have been set beside the front or rear kitchen window[257] with a chair at either end. When the family were having a meal, other chairs placed about the kitchen could be put around the table to accommodate all the members. Much of the washing up was done on such a table near a window.

Chairs

In the early days chairs in Irish kitchens were often rope-seated; later—as in the Dunfanaghy region—they were usually of solid wooden construction and locally made from pine (in the nineteenth and twentieth centuries) to a simple and sturdy design (straight legs and back with a flat seat, or 'stickback' types) [see e.g. Pls 77, 86b]. Later still, in the twentieth century, beechwood chairs with railed backs and hollowed seats began to be bought, sometimes purchased with coupons issued by itinerant vendors of tea.

By the fire, the three-legged stool—the so-called 'creepie'—was also in evidence,[258] standing firm on an uneven floor. Such stools were also used as milking stools [Pl. 91]. Low benches of simple construction—'forms'— were also common in the Dunfanaghy region [Pl. 92a–b], often set out at right angles from the fire, as well as larger free-standing wooden settles which were used both as seats and as extra beds [Pl. 93].

Other kitchen equipment and features

Cooking in the rural Donegal kitchen was done either in a cast-iron flat-bottomed pot (the 'pot oven', often used for baking bread) or, more commonly, in the famous three-legged metal pot (of varying size) suspended over the fire on the crane[259] [see Pl. 87b]. Typical also was the round-bellied cast-iron kettle, similarly suspended from the crane.

It was an Irish custom to keep most of the dairying equipment in the kitchen. This included upright wooden churns, which occupied a place against a wall, usually opposite the fire.[260] The shape of the stave-built upright plunge churn differed regionally in Ireland,[261] but in basic design the lid had a hole through which the churn 'dash' passed, terminating in a wooden cross at the bottom[262] [Pl. 94]. The kitchen or living-room of the Donegal cottage would also have had a clock. In the Dunfanaghy region the commonest type was of the 'Black Forest' variety with a pendulum[263]

Pl. 67a—A traditional two-sash cottage window, with two panes per sash.

Pl. 67b—Another well-preserved example of a traditional two-sash window.

Pl. 67c—(Below left) The small windows' openings—as here—were often 'chamfered' internally so as to let in more light.

Pl. 67d—(Below right) Another example of a chamfered window opening—here made of unmortared local slaty stone.

[Pl. 95]. It was usual also for religious items to have a special place on the wall or on a shelf in the main living-room [Pl. 96], including one or more 'Brigid's crosses' hanging on the wall[264] [Pl. 97a–b]. Perhaps the most important of the religious items was the Sacred Heart lamp, which was usually made of brass and was either hung on the wall or set on a stand on the table. Usually, though, it would hang on the wall under the picture of the Sacred Heart and be kept alight at all times. When the main lamp in the kitchen was extinguished, the little lamp provided a useful dim background light in the kitchen throughout the night.

The bedroom

As has been seen, after the initial 'byre-dwelling' layout went out of fashion, corridor-less separate bedrooms—with a step up—were added on one or both sides of the original unit, with internal interconnecting doors of sheeted timber.

As mentioned above, in the Dunfanaghy region large rooms (whether kitchen or bedroom) were often subdivided with partitions in later times to give further small bed units, sometimes side by side along the back wall [Pl. 98a]. This was in addition to any 'outshot' bed niche in the kitchen or any curtained-off sleeping area there (see above). The partitioning was usually of matching board construction, but in earlier times wattle partitioning may have been used, constructed of timber frames with strips of bog fir nailed across them and then plastered with locally quarried lime (the lime-kilns used for such purposes are still much in evidence in the region of study). The half-inch strips of fir were cut from the bog timber with a special tool called an 'etch' when the timber was newly taken from the bog and was still soft. Strips could then be pulled off along the grain with the etch. Stand-alone or built-in wardrobes were used in later times for storing clothes [Pl. 98b].

The surviving beds in the region appear to be of the iron-framed variety. Most bedrooms in the area have their own fire grates surrounded by a wooden mantlepiece [see Pl. 85a–b].

A common item in the bedrooms of old cottages was a trunk or large suitcase—most households then contained at least one member of the family who had been to America or Britain and then returned. These trunks made handy containers for storing sheets, blankets or clothing that was not worn very often, as well as other knick-knacks, such as important

Pl. 67e—(Top left) An example of a rear two-sash window, smaller than those in the front and having a single pane to each sash.

Pl. 67f—(Top right) Local cottage windows were traditionally surmounted by a large slate lintel, as here.

Pl. 68a—(Left) A rare example of an upper window in a local cottage.

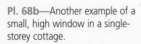

Pl. 68b—Another example of a small, high window in a single-storey cottage.

papers or documents and photos. The trunks would be made of timber with a rounded top and measured about 3ft long by 2ft high [Pl. 99a].

Internal decoration

As on the outside, so also the internal walls of the Donegal cottage were generally limewashed[265] [Pls 74, 99b]. A common feature, however, in the Dunfanaghy region is for the lower walls of kitchens to be painted a dark colour, only the upper half being whitewashed, with a decorative border in between.[266]

Floors

The floors of Irish cottages would originally have been made from compressed earth, and in the older cottages and outhouses in the Dunfanaghy area the local so-called 'blue clay' was used[267] [Pl. 100]. (This was also used locally in times past to wrap up wild game birds for cooking in the open fire!) When compressed and dried, this clay looks like cement. In later times large local (Roshine) slates—mined from the deeper quarry layers—were used as flagstones in living-rooms in the region; usually grey but sometimes white, they were laid out in roughly interlocking patterns over the whole floor space[268] [Pl. 101]. Local wisdom used to have it that when the flags starting 'sweating' (going black with condensation) wet weather was on the way (or had already arrived!).

Lighting

In the Irish cottage, lighting was most needed in the kitchen around the fire,[269] where originally there would have been a 'hob-lamp'. The earliest lights were of the 'crusie' variety, consisting of a dried rush or wick in an open oil container. Later the candle and the paraffin lamp, including the famous 'Tilley', took over. Remants of these can still be seen in a few cottages in the Dunfanaghy region, including a candle lantern [Pl. 102].

Pl. 69—A typical wooden partition of a large room in a Donegal cottage. Note that the boarding does not extend upwards as far as ceiling height.

Pl. 70—(Above) An example of more permanent partitioning (now removed) at the back of a large room to make extra sleeping places.

Pl. 71—(Above) Here a dresser is set out at a right angle to the kitchen wall to form a curtained-off alcove for additional sleeping space.

Pl. 72—(Right) Another example of a curtained-off sleeping space in the kitchen of a cottage at Derryreel.

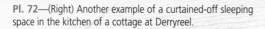

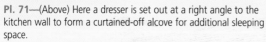

Sanitation

Toilet facilities in the old Donegal cottage were originally non-existent,[270] except for the portable 'potty'. It seems to have been traditional for women to use the byre and men the stable.[271]

Pl. 73—(Left) Here the ceiling line of the room extends up to the roof ridge, giving emphasis to the two exposed original bog timber purlins.

Pl. 74—(Below) The kitchen of a former traditional cottage at Horn Head, where the ceiling was open to the smoke-blackened Roshine slates (see left-hand corner). Note also the rippled effect of the lime mortar on the walls.

Pl. 75—(Below left) A rare surviving example of a high wall door to give access to the roof space beyond, often as an extra sleeping compartment.

Pl. 76—(Below right) An example of a small pantry room adjacent to a kitchen.

OUTHOUSES, ETC.

As discussed above, after the demise of the 'byre-dwelling', farm outhouses in Donegal were often set out side by side in a single line (the extended 'longhouse'),[272] where cattle and other animals were housed in separate units from those of human habitation but under the same roof. Added to the gable of the house, the roof line of such byres is often lower, or in some cases higher (as in the case of an added hayloft—a byre with a barn above[273]). If not attached to the dwelling units, outhouses in clusters or free-standing groups were built opposite the latter or parallel to them[274] across the walkway (the 'street'), often stretching in a line of units [Pl. 103a, d] purpose-built for each type of animal or fowl kept (e.g. pigsties and *cróite* ('craws') for hens, ducks and geese, including special niches under the steps of lofts for such fowl[275]) [Pl. 103b] or in haphazard positions near the house [Pl. 103c]. An outbuilding for the farm cart was also common. Larger animals such as horses and cattle were normally housed in the nearer byres attached to the dwelling. Some outbuildings— so-called 'boiling houses'—in the Dunfanaghy region have a small gable chimney for taking smoke from a fire under a pot used for boiling up potatoes for cattle or hen feed [Pl. 104], and some also featured a threshing machine powered by the farm horse [see Pl. 24].

Originally thatched, towards the end of the nineteenth century many such outbuildings came to be slated, felted or tinned.[276] When tinned and painted with the red or green roofing paint, they are a pleasant complement to the older roof types. Often the flooring of outhouses consisted of flags, with a stone-lined open drain sloping down in the centre.[277]

Any paved or stone-lined area in front of a Donegal cottage was usually known, somewhat grandiosely, as 'the street'[278] [see Pl. 103a], and in the Dunfanaghy region it is not uncommon to find a small area outside the front door paved with flags [see e.g. Pls 29, 59a]. In the 'street' there might be a specially built channel running down the slope from the front door—similar to the runnel in the middle of byres—for carrying away waste water from the kitchen. This was composed (in one surviving example near Dunfanaghy) of long squarish stones set end to end on both sides, with cobblestones inside [Pl. 105].

Lastly, as seen, at the entrance to the boreen leading to the Donegal cottage rounded gate pillars, often whitewashed, are typical[279][Pl. 105].

Pl. 77—A still-inhabited old cottage which, unusually, has a fireplace with protruding breastwork around it.

Pl. 78a—(Below left) A typical feature of local cottages—flues blanked off above the fire by use of flagstones placed end-on in an ascending line, and often rendered over with mortar to match the rest of the wall.

Pl. 78b—(Above right) Another example of a slated chimney flue set above the original crane.

Pl. 78c—Large flue slates set lengthways, and resting on small buttresses of stone.

SELECT BIBLIOGRAPHY

Aalen, F. 1970 The house types of Gola Island, Co. Donegal. *Folk Life* **8**, 32–44.

Boyle, D. 1998 *A sense of loss: the survival of rural traditional buildings in Northern Ireland*. Environment and Heritage Service, NI.

Danaher, K. 1975 *Ireland's vernacular architecture*. Cork. Mercier Press.

Evans, E. 1957 *Irish folk ways*. London. Routledge and Kegan Paul.

Gailey, A. 1979 Vernacular housing in north-west Ulster. In A. Rowan, *North-west Ulster*, 87–103. Middlesex. Penguin.

Gailey, A. 1984 *Rural houses of the north of Ireland*. Edinburgh. John Donald.

Geography in Action Website: *Vernacular housing of the Inishowen Peninsula*: www.geographyinaction.co.uk (website dealing with vernacular housing in County Donegal).

Hannan, R. and Bell, J. 2000 The bothog; a seasonal dwelling from Co. Donegal. In T.M. Owen (ed.), *From Corrib to Cultra*, 71–81. Belfast. Institute of Irish Studies.

Lysaght, P. 1994 Vernacular rural dwellings in Ireland. In B. Ni Fhloinn and G. Dennison (eds), *Traditional architecture in Ireland and its role in rural development and tourism*, 8–20. Dublin. UCD.

McCourt, D. 1965 Some cruck-framed buildings in Donegal and Derry. *Ulster Folklife* **11**, 39–50.

McCourt, D. 1970 The house with bedroom over byre: a long-house derivative? *Ulster Folklife* **15/16**, 3–19.

Mullane, F. 2000 Vernacular architecture. In N. Buttimer, C. Rynne and H. Guerin, *The heritage of Ireland*, 71–9. Cork. Collins Press.

Ó Danachair, C. 1945 The questionnaire system [on roofing and thatching]. *Béaloidas* **15**, 203–17.

Ó Danachair, C. 1964 The combined byre-and-dwelling in Ireland. *Folk Life* **2**, 58–75.

O'Reilly, B. 2004 *Living under thatch*. Cork. Mercier Press.

Pfeiffer, W. and Shaffrey, M. 1990 *Irish cottages*. London. Weidenfeld and Nicholson.

Pritchard, D. 1998 *The Irish cottage*. Real Ireland Design Ltd.

Ulster Architectural Heritage Society 2000 *Buildings at risk*. Environment and Heritage Service, NI.

Ulster Folk and Transport Museum 1979 *Magheragallan byre houses* (the 'Cultra leaflet').

Pl. 79—A sideways-on shot showing the typically outward-slanting slate at the bottom of a flue resting each side on a small buttress of cantilevered stone.

Pl. 80—A curious example of a flueway from the kitchen fire being diverted to connect with the flue of a bedroom above in a two-storey cottage.

Pl. 81a—A simple stone lintel over a fire opening.

Pl. 81b—Another example of a stone lintel over a small bedroom fire.

NOTES

(1)   In respect of what has been described as the largely 'undocumented cultural materials' of the Irish countryside outside the six counties (Gailey 1984, v—hence the importance (*ibid.*) of fitting documentary evidence into the 'oral testimony' of those who lived in vernacular houses). In fact there exist few records of any kind on the more humble vernacular houses 'at any period' (*ibid.*, 27). Donegal County Council itself has recently acknowledged that 'additional research is required' in the area of 'vernacular buildings', for which it would seek 'funding under the Heritage Grants Scheme' (see note 20 below).

(2)   Cf. Gailey 1984, 12. Mullane (2000, 71, 75) points out that information collection on vernacular architecture has been 'largely unsystematic' and by individuals rather than by 'survey teams'. She also makes the point (*op. cit.*, 75), very relevant to the present study (where the cottages have roofs of local slate), that research on *this type* of vernacular building style has been neglected.

(3)   Boyle 1998, n. 4, sections 2.05, 6.01.

(4)   Boyle 1998.

(5)   See Aalen 1970, 32 (a longhouse may be defined as 'an elongated building intended to house men and animals together, with internal access' and 'usually it contains a dwelling area at one end and accommodation for livestock at the other').

(6)   Pfeiffer and Shaffrey 1990, 14. As they add, they also provided homes for 'large numbers of people over the centuries' (*ibid.*, 143).

(7)   *Ibid.*, 14.

(8)   Evans 1957, 39, quoting the words of Robin Flower (*The Western Isle* (1944), 46).

(9)   Evans 1957, 40. In a recently published book on vernacular thatched cottages in Ireland, O'Reilly (2004, 13) makes the same point and adds an interesting list of differences between 'vernacular architecture' and 'formal architecture'.

(10)   'In search of the typical', *Irish Times*, March 2000.

(11)   Pfeiffer and Shaffrey 1990, 105.

(12)   Evans 1957, 21.

(13)   See more generally O'Reilly 2004, 65, on such effects of the loss of traditional rural cottages ('[a] degraded landscape has little attraction for the tourist').

(14)   Pfeiffer and Shaffrey 1990, 14.

(15)   See Boyle 1998, section 1.10.

(16)   Obviously the availability of improvement grants would assist in this (see e.g. Gailey 1984, 242–3, who mentions the straitjacket of confined accommodation in many one-storey vernacular buildings, with windows of limited size and no bathrooms, where modernisation should be permitted to encourage continued occupation with a full range of modern conveniences; and that provided that damp problems may be overcome, the typically thick mass walls of such cottages are thermally efficient).

(17)   See Pl. 4a.

(18)   Several questions have been raised in the Dáil over this problem: see e.g.

Pl. 82—A partly slate-fronted fireplace complete with the original crane and attachments.

Pl. 83—A slightly raised hearth, with the traditional three-legged pot hanging from the crane.

Pl. 84—One of the last remaining examples in County Donegal of an old 'Stanley-type' range still in daily use.

Dáil Debates, vol. 506, col. 104, where a grant scheme for conservation of protected buildings, administered by local authorities, is mentioned as having been launched in May 1999. See also vol. 510, col. 1308 (16 November 1999) (no official plans to 'introduce a generally available grant scheme' for refurbishment of derelict buildings in rural areas).

(19)   See e.g. *Dáil Debates*, vol. 503, col. 1355 (27 April 1999).

(20)   See *Record of Protected Structures: response and recommendations to submissions made during public consultation process* (Donegal County Council, 18 November 2003), 4: 'The Conservation Officer will play a pivotal role in the implementation of the Record of Protected Structures by providing a specialist services [*sic*] to owners/occupiers preparing declarations under Section 57 of the Local Government (Planning and Development) Act, 2000, promoting the importance of conserving our built heritage among local communities and investigating sources of funding to maximise the opportunities for owners/occupiers'.

(21)   *Ibid.*; very few vernacular cottages are included in the listing (apparently only three—at Cardonagh, Malin Head and Mountcharles).

(22)   The same situation appears to have pertained in Northern Ireland: cf. Boyle 1998, section 1.08 (a bias towards allowing new buildings where old buildings already existed).

(23)   See the letter of one of the authors to the *Irish Times* of 5 October 1999.

(24)   The Planning and Development Act, 2000, which provides for 'protected structures'.

(25)   The experience in Northern Ireland has parallels: see Boyle 1998, where it was found that vernacular buildings in rural areas tended to be under-represented in early surveys, and that (worse still) there had been a serious loss of these traditional buildings since the late 1970s (executive summary)—the traditional stone houses and farm buildings of Ulster not being generally seen to qualify as being 'of special architectural or historic interest', unless, possibly, they had thatched roofs (section 1.03). The situation in Northern Ireland thus seems to have been comparable in terms of the legislative problems in the Republic, i.e. the ease of obtaining planning permission to replace old dwellings, with regulations insisting on demolition of the older structure if permission for a replacement house is granted. This planning policy obviously does not favour 'retention of vernacular buildings' (see Ulster Architectural Heritage Society 2000, 38).

(26)   Many such cottages are in any case now hardly distinguishable from genuine 'byres' where bungalows have been built in front of or around them.

(27)   Personal communication of 11 May 2001 from Donegal County Council to one of the authors. The County Donegal Draft Development Plan (1998) (vol. 1 at p. 62) had optimistically stated that the Council would complete an inventory of buildings of architectural, historic or artistic importance by the year 2000. Material Alteration (No. 1) to the Draft Plan (1998) did advocate (p. 4) 'reuse of existing rundown and derelict houses and outbuildings where possible'; and (p. 6), in landscape categories 1 and 2, that single holiday homes should be permitted through 'renovation of a derelict or rundown structure'; and (p. 7) that 'refurbishment of intact but rundown buildings/structures which are of significant architectural,

Pl. 85a—A typical bedroom fireplace in north Donegal.

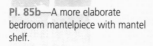

Pl. 85b—A more elaborate bedroom mantelpiece with mantel shelf.

historical interest' would be considered in landscape category 3 for permanent or holiday rental usage.

(28)   The two old inhabitants were eventually provided with an adjacent 'Portacabin', where both lived until their respective deaths.

(29)   Pfeiffer and Shaffrey 1990, 91.

(30)   Cf. Danaher 1975, 79 (old dwellings may descend down the social scale, so that 'yesterday's dwelling-house becomes today's cattle byre'). See also Gailey (1984, 241), who notes that, in south-west Donegal, development often took the form of building a new dwelling in front of an old one. The result is that the old structures stand 'like ghosts in the shadows of new houses' (Introduction by Alice Taylor in Pfeiffer and Shaffrey 1990, 12).

(31)   Gailey (1984, 243) mentions that misguided attempts at modernisation include the installation of picture windows, flat-roofed porches, etc., which all 'detract from the "feel" of the vernacular'; and he describes examples of unsympathetic treatment of traditional houses in Northern Ireland as 'numerous'.

(32)   See, for example, Pfeiffer and Shaffrey 1990, 14, 72; Gailey 1984, 8.

(33)   Gailey 1984, 8.

(34)   *Ibid.*, 33.

(35)   *Ibid.*, 224.

(36)   Evans 1957, 41.

(37)   Gailey 1984, 10.

(38)   Two such byre-cottages (one intact and in use until 1950, the other in ruins) were removed from Magheragallan on the north-west coast of County Donegal near Derrybeg and reconstructed at the Ulster Folk and Transport Museum at Cultra in Northern Ireland. The internal measurements of the entire house were 26ft by 15ft, the thick walls being of (mostly) granite boulders, with a typical rounded roof profile for thatch (see below, note 127), and stone pegs under the eaves for roping down. In fact a width of 15ft for small Donegal cottages seems typical.

(39)   Pffeifer and Shaffrey 1990, 17. In its 'most basic form'—'common in north-western and western parts' of Ireland—a 'humble one-room dwelling was sometimes shared by animals', such houses having a sloping drain to 'discharge effluent' (*ibid.*, 17–18).

(40)   Gailey 1984, 142, 144.

(41)   Such houses could produce physical discomfort and pollution from animal manure (about a ton and a half after winter in the Gweedore area—Cultra leaflet, 1979).

(42)   Danaher 1975, 70. The Cultra leaflet (referring to the content of note 38 above) mentions a well-marked stone drain separating house end from byre end, with no physical separation between man and beast, and shows a photo of a byre end which would have been big enough to house about three cattle.

(43)   Quoted by Estyn Evans (1957, 40).

(44)   *Ibid.*, 41.

(45)   *Ibid.*, 86.

(46)   According to the Cultra leaflet. See also Ó Danachair 1964, 59, where it is mentioned that inspectors from the Congested Districts Board at the end of the nineteenth century stated that a combined dwelling and byre was common in parts of Donegal.

Pl. 86a—A typical Donegal 'crane', used for swinging pots over the open fire.

Pl. 86b—Another, more elaborate, example of a fireside crane.

(47) Gailey 1984, 142.
(48) As the Cultra leaflet says, the nineteenth-century social changes meant that the byre came to be separated from the house by a wall that went to roof height, but sometimes with an internal connecting door giving access to the byre. See also Aalen 1970, 39: '[a] major step in the modification of the internal [longhouse] plan was the division of the family living area into two rooms', the inner room usually being for the womenfolk.
(49) Evans 1957, 44.
(50) As has been said, 'the term "long house" could not be more appropriate in Donegal as the extended [linear] house can go on forever: dwelling, byre and hayloft, stable, dairy, store, piggery etc.', the dwelling and outbuildings often being in one continuous line enclosed by the same walls and covered by the same unbroken roof (Pffeifer and Shaffrey 1990, 27 and 84).
(51) Gailey 1984, 10.
(52) *Ibid.,* 145.
(53) See Gailey 1984, 170 ('many three-unit dwellings had their roof lines continued over separately entered stores and outhouses', possibly with internal connecting doors).
(54) Danaher 1975, 70.
(55) Pfeiffer and Shaffrey 1990, 17.
(56) The smaller version of the linear cottage had only a kitchen and bedroom, 'with sleeping accommodation set against the hearth wall and warmed by it' (Pfeiffer and Shaffrey 1990, 17).
(57) Gailey 1984, 145. So where a house was extended to three or more units, the kitchen unit was commonly away from the gable ends (*ibid.,* 160). His diagrams illustrate how added outhouses could extend along the long axis of the building in the north-west of Ireland (*ibid.,* 233).
(58) The room behind the chimney was often known as 'the room'. It could be used for other purposes than simply sleeping; for example, one such (end) room in the Symmons-owned cottage was reputedly used for taking the so-called 'stations', i.e. for celebrating occasional 'in-house' Masses, when the local priest would visit and local inhabitants would congregate there for the purpose.
(59) See the Cultra leaflet, *Magheragallan byre-house,* published by the Ulster Folk and Transport Museum in 1979.
(60) See Pfeiffer and Shaffrey 1990, 30.
(61) *Ibid.,* 26.
(62) Gailey 1984, 160–1.
(63) *Ibid.,* 9.
(64) *Ibid.,* 10.
(65) Pfeiffer and Shaffrey 1990, 27.
(66) Gailey 1984, 191. For him, the term 'bays' applied to distances between roof-trusses on gables or internal walls 'rising to roof-ridge height' (*ibid.,* 33–4).
(67) As the Cultra leaflet says, improved standards of comfort and hygiene in rural communities led to a physical separation between dwelling area and byre. See also Gailey 1984, 145.
(68) See the Cultra leaflet and *Vernacular housing of the Inishowen Peninsula* (the separation by a solid wall of a byre from the main living area often

Pl. 87a—A close-up of a variety of pot-hanging hooks.

Pl. 87b—(Below) A repositioned crane in an old cottage on which traditional cooking utensils have been hung and below which stands an old bread oven (for baking bread in the turf ashes).

Pl. 87c—(Below left) A wood-lined 'keeping-hole' by a fire.

Pl. 87d—(Below right) Another example of a 'keeping-hole'.

'allowed the room where the byre would have been to become a bedroom'); and Aalen 1970, 40 ('gradual modification for human uses of space traditionally allocated for livestock accommodation').

(69)   Gailey 1984, 144.

(70)   On former dwelling areas being later converted to outhouses see Gailey 1984, 234.

(71)   *Ibid.*, 1.

(72)   See e.g. Pfeiffer and Shaffrey 1990, 19; Gailey (1984, 76) suggests that representation of a vernacular building on the 1834 Ordnance Survey map may indicate probable construction at the end of the eighteenth century or in the early nineteenth century.

(73)   Gailey 1984, 7. Most particularly, the availability of local materials imposed its stamp on the local design and construction of such dwellings (as in the case of breadth). As Gailey adds (*op. cit.*, 14), dating such buildings in Ireland is often impossible because of the 'very slow pace of design change at vernacular level'.

(74)   *Ibid.*, 70.

(75)   *Ibid.*, 75.

(76)   As Gailey (1984, 27) says, because 'many men had helped someone else build a dwelling . . . essential techniques were widely known' and, of course, passed on.

(77)   Cited by Estyn Evans (1957, 57).

(78)   *Ibid.*

(79)   *Ibid.*, 225.

(80)   Evans 1957, 11–12.

(81)   *Ibid.*, 21.

(82)   Gailey 1984, 225. The reconstructed cottage at Cultra was built at Magheragallan in the second half of the nineteenth century as part of a cluster close to shore, originally owned by folk from inland townlands who brought cattle for grazing on the sandhills—a sort of 'booleying' co-operative!

(83)   As one of the writers was informed by the former inhabitant of the farm, this situation led to friction amongst the adults when he was a child.

(84)   See e.g. Pfeiffer and Shaffrey 1990, 78; Lysaght 1994, 9.

(85)   Evans 1957, 31.

(86)   As in a now-restored cottage in Roshine. The present owners have since dug away the bank and put down storm drains!

(87)   Pfeiffer and Shaffrey 1990, 33.

(88)   Evans 1957, 111, 112.

(89)   Cited by Gailey (1984, 227).

(90)   See e.g. Pfeiffer and Shaffrey 1990, 33; Gailey 1984, 226.

(91)   See, for example, the photograph in Gailey 1984 at p. 149; see also note 279 below.

(92)   Pffeiffer and Shaffrey 1990, 18.

(93)   Extensions in line were common, often to incorporate a range of outbuildings: see Pfeiffer and Shaffrey 1990, 28, 30 (lean-to), 90 (long).

(94)   See Gailey 1984, 229.

(95)   Evans 1957, 112.

(96)   McCourt (1970, 3) points out that the axis of byre additions was often 'aligned down a slope' so that one end of the building would be higher

Pl. 88—A typical wall-recessed cupboard.

Pl. 89—An example of a wall-hung cup rack in an old north Donegal kitchen.

Pl. 90a—(Below left) A typical Donegal cottage dresser (this one is still in use!).

Pl. 90b—(Below right) Such dressers were often brightly painted, as is this one.

and built into a bank.

(97)   Gailey 1984, 33.

(98)   For example, one small Roshine cottage has rafters measuring *c.* 9in. by 2in.

(99)   For example, in one ruined Roshine cottage the two main rooms are respectively 18ft and 15ft long, and both 15ft wide; another small cottage there has main rooms 12ft and 15ft long respectively, and 15ft wide. Other small cottages in the region are only 12–15ft wide.

(100)   Gailey (1984, 48) describes the various sources of vernacular stone for Irish cottages, rectangular shapes being used for corners, sills, window dressings, etc., and the walls being built of coursed rubble or 'uncoursed' (*ibid.*, 78). Such stone construction was by the eighteenth century common even in the case of early 'byre-dwellings' in west Donegal (on the use of rounded boulders with platy stone as packing, see his photo at p. 50).

(101)   *Ibid.*, 62, 63.

(102)   Gailey (1984, 52) points out that bonding with lime mortar goes back to the seventeenth century and persisted into the nineteenth century.

(103)   See Pfeiffer and Shaffrey 1990, 90.

(104)   Gailey 1984, 63.

(105)   *Ibid.*, 63.

(106)   According to the Cultra leaflet.

(107)   Gailey 1984, 63.

(108)   Pfeiffer and Shaffrey 1990, 76.

(109)   Gailey 1984, 64.

(110)   See e.g. Danaher (1975, 14), who says that the limewashing of outer walls and the use of local materials gives a 'high degree of environmental harmony'. In the light of the 'bungalow blitz' which has hit County Donegal and the ongoing disappearance of old cottages, Pffeifer and Shaffrey's comment (even in the early 1990s) to the effect that '[a]ll over Donegal limewashed houses vie with each other in their crisp, gleaming whiteness' (1990, 18) seems now to be sadly untrue and misplaced.

(111)   Pfeiffer and Shaffrey 1990, 105 ('The custom is to whitewash [the cottages] annually, even in the most remote places').

(112)   *Ibid.*, 16, 18, 98.

(113)   *Ibid.*, 98.

(114)   Gailey 1984, 243.

(115)   As Pfeiffer and Shaffrey note (1990, 18), gable windows were never used on the 'ground floor'.

(116)   Pfeiffer and Shaffrey 1990, 83.

(117)   See Evans 1957, 48.

(118)   Pfeiffer and Shaffrey 1990, 30. They say that during the nineteenth century and earlier a large number of slate quarries operated in Ireland (*ibid.*, 88); see also Gailey (1984, 110), who mentions slate mines in County Donegal. The roof slope was usually 45–50%: Danaher 1975, 52–3.

(119)   See e.g. Pfeiffer and Shaffrey 1990, 72; Gailey 1984, 66; Danaher 1975, 54.

(120)   See Gailey 1984, 109.

(121)   See Pfeiffer and Shaffrey 1990, 88.

(122)   Danaher 1975, 57.

(123)   Pfeiffer and Shaffrey 1990, 88, 90.

Pl. 91—A traditional three-legged stool.

Pl. 92a—(Above) A typical Donegal small seat bench.

Pl. 92b—(Left) Another example of a simply constructed seat bench.

(124) Another source of local slates was said to be a mine in St Johnston, in the east of the county.

(125) Evans 1957, 48.

(126) Undoubtedly, as Gailey (1984, 94) points out more generally, the presence of nearby slate quarries could account for the decrease of thatched buildings in a particular area.

(127) Unlike slated roofs, which have a pointed apex, thatched roofs in the Dunfanaghy region and elsewhere in Ireland are typically rounded at the ridge to combat winds: see generally Pfeiffer and Shaffrey 1990, 83–4.

(128) As in other parts of Ireland, choice of thatching material depended on what was available locally (Gailey 1984, 95).

(129) I have been unable to locate this word in an Irish dictionary, and it seems to have only a very localised usage even in County Donegal. It is noteworthy that Ó Danachair (1945, 208) expressly mentions 'certain tough grasses' often being used in mountainous parts of Donegal.

(130) See Gailey 1984, 46 and 93; Evans 1957, 50.

(131) See Gailey 1984, 92.

(132) Gailey (1984, 100) points out that the thatch in west and north County Donegal was almost always secured by a 'close grid of ropes' both horizontal and vertical (*ibid.*, 96 and 103).

(133) One reconstructed cottage at Cultra (see note 38 above) has marram grass over scraws, and a series of ropes which were originally hand-twisted crossing from side to side and tied to stone pegs under the eaves, with 'longitudinal ropes' lying underneath to prevent cutting into the thatch.

(134) One of the authors personally witnessed this procedure in his younger days!

(135) See e.g. Pfeiffer and Shaffrey 1990, 84 ('pegs below the eaves'), and Danaher 1975, 55 (the ropes were attached to gable or eave). Sometimes in north-west Donegal the ropes were used vertically only with a stone at the end, the rope ends only later being tied to pegs in wall heads, such as projecting stones: Gailey 1984, 103; Ó Danachair 1945, 211.

(136) See Gailey 1984, 95.

(137) Inasmuch as corrugated iron reputedly goes back to Victorian times, it can be said to be almost 'vernacular' roofing; it is described by Pritchard (1998) as deserving 'more respect than it receives from modern planners and architects' and as 'almost as attractive a roofing material as thatch and much easier to maintain'.

(138) See Pfeiffer and Shaffrey 1990, 24 (the dwelling could be extended and 'partly raised', so that an extended section could break through the roof line of an earlier single-storey construction).

(139) See e.g. Pfeiffer and Shaffrey 1990, 24, 26, 34 (byres at each end are often of lower height), and Gailey 1984, 160 (often only one unit was carried upwards, the others retaining single-storey status).

(140) Aalen (1970, 43) notes that on the Donegal island of Gola there are some two-storey byres, the upper byre being used as a granary or hayloft.

(141) Gailey 1984, 93.

(142) Gailey (1984, 90) says that purlin roofs would have been common in vernacular houses in the north-west from at least the mid-eighteenth century onwards, mortices and tenons being rare.

(143) Gailey 1984, 71. Evans (1957, 13) says that the rural population turned to

Pl. 93—A typical wooden settle bench.

Pl. 94—A local butter churn.

Pl. 95—An example of a common north Donegal cottage wall clock (of the 'Black Forest' design).

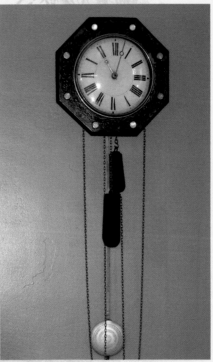

the 'fossil oak and pine of the bogs' after the destruction of the native forests by the seventeenth century. The result was that in the late eighteenth and early nineteenth centuries, 'as settlement was pushed into poorer localities often higher in the hills,... because suitable growing timber no longer existed in the countryside, fossil timber from peat bogs came into increasing use' (Gailey 1984, 33).

(144) Cited by Gailey (1984, 72).

(145) Gailey 1984, 80. He particularly mentions such an example at Horn Head, which, of course, is in the Dunfanaghy area.

(146) Plate 54 shows clearly the use of wooden pegs to join the timbers together without the use of nails. McCourt (1965, 46) mentions that cruck trusses in County Donegal are usually to be found in narrow byres rather than in dwelling-houses, suggesting that they 'represent the last lingering traces of a tradition which [in County Donegal and probably elsewhere] died out much earlier'.

(147) Gailey 1984, 91.

(148) *Ibid.*, 88. Gailey also refers (p. 83) to the truss feet being carried (presumably for extra strength) 'on stone pads corbelled out from the inner wall faces at or just below wall height' or (p. 91) on 'buttresses' on the inside of walls. For diagrams of basic roof types, see Gailey 1984, 73, fig. 69.

(149) Danaher (1975, 52) shows a diagram of a roof space with short collar-brace—a roof type found, he says, in County Donegal.

(150) Gailey 1984, 88. His fig. 86 (p. 89) shows a byre-dwelling like this in Donegal. As a variation, a longer yoke might carry the ridge purlin and a side purlin at each of its ends (*ibid.*, 90).

(151) Evans 1957, 52. See the Donegal 'byre' roof in Pl. 54, where the top yoke is jointed into the back of two supporting trusses fixed with two wooden pegs to the same (some still protruding), all of rough-hewn bog fir. The second tie-beam below is fixed with single pegs to a truss and the bottom tie-beam jointed into trusses above the wallplate with double pegs. The bottoms of both trusses rest on the wallplate.

(152) See McCourt 1965, 48.

(153) See Gailey 1984, 74.

(154) See the leaflet on the reconstruction at Cultra.

(155) Ascribable to the late eighteenth century or later: see Gailey 1984, 90.

(156) *Ibid.*

(157) *Ibid.*, 91.

(158) In the case of the reconstructed cottage at Cultra, the roof timbers were of sawn wood, much of which could have been collected along the Donegal shore.

(159) With such purlins only a few runs were needed on each side of the roof.

(160) See Danagher 1957, 92–3.

(161) Evans (1957, 48) notes that when slates are used for roofing 'old roof patterns are faithfully followed by local builders'; the diminishing 'row size' feature of the study area seems to go back a long way, as all surviving slated roofs there seem to show this.

(162) Gailey 1984, 8. See also Pfeiffer and Shaffrey 1990, 30–72 (stacks on the 'ridge').

(163) See e.g. Pfeiffer and Shaffrey 1990, 84.

Pl. 96—A typical religious picture on a cottage wall-shelf.

Pl. 97a—The most common St Brigid's cross in north Donegal.

Pl. 97b—A variant pattern of the St Brigid's cross.

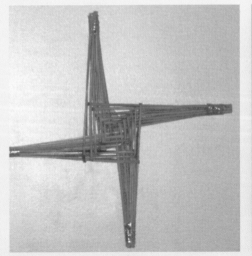

(164) Gailey 1984, 140.
(165) See Pfeiffer and Shaffrey 1990, 16; Gailey 1984, 151 ('Most outshots were roofed externally merely by continuing the house roof outwards, but in a few cases a small separate roof was necessary').
(166) See Gailey 1984, 19 and 140. He says that they are to be found in counties Donegal, Derry, Antrim, Tyrone, north Fermanagh, north Leitrim and Sligo (*ibid.*, 156). Evans (1957, 71) suggests that the feature may attest to contacts with western Scotland. A survey by the Irish Folklore Commission in the mid-1930s highlighted this as a special north-western feature (Lysaght 1994, 8). See also Lysaght 1994, 13, 14 ('a genuine traditional element of the domestic building culture of the region').
(167) See Gailey 1984, 144 and 215 ('rear corner next to the hearth').
(168) *Ibid.*, 151.
(169) Evans 1957, 69. Gailey (1984, 153, 213) shows plans of houses with outshots in the corner nearest the fire.
(170) Evans 1957, 71. He also comments (p. 88) that, placed against one of the side walls near the fire, the settle-bed 'admirably illustrates the economy of space and function characteristic of Irish kitchen furnishings'. Cf. Gailey 1984, 151 ('internally it enlarged the living space so that the bed it accommodated impinged as little as possible, if at all, on the kitchen floor area').
(171) Gailey 1984, 156 (it was instead a 'genuine, traditional element in the housing of northern and southern Ireland').
(172) According to Gailey (1984, 151), they vary from 15cm to about 80cm deep.
(173) Thus one Roshine cottage has two outshots, one in each of the main rooms; one is only about six inches deep, whilst the other is two and a half feet deep. In the case of the reconstructed 'byre' cottages at Cultra there is evidence of a slight outshot in the entire cottage and a 'full' ('true') outshot in the ruined one (see leaflet).
(174) See *Vernacular housing of the Inishowen Peninsula*, 4.
(175) Gailey 1984, 151.
(176) *Ibid.*, 215–16; Evans 1957, 87.
(177) See Pfeiffer and Shaffrey 1990, 16; Gailey 1984, 151–6.
(178) Evans 1957, 87.
(179) But Gailey (1984, 155) has a photo of a cottage in Tyrone which does have a tiny window in the outshot.
(180) See Pfeiffer and Shaffrey 1990, 16 and 19. Gailey (1984, 131) mentions them as being sometimes roofed separately (though thatched roofs could extend down to them), late examples often having a miniature slated roof.
(181) See *Vernacular housing of the Inishowen Peninsula*, 8.
(182) Gailey 1984, 84.
(183) *Ibid.*, 218.
(184) For example, in one Roshine cottage the porch extends out for only 2ft, the two walls being *c.* 1ft 6in. thick.
(185) Gailey 1984, 223.
(186) See, more generally, Evans 1957, 100.
(187) Gailey 1984, 131; Pfeiffer and Shaffrey 1990, 28.
(188) Pfeiffer and Shaffrey 1990, 11, 16.

Pl. 98a—(Left) A now-ruinous example of simple partitioning of part of an existing large room to provide extra bedrooms.

Pl. 98b—(Right) A crude 'built-in' wardrobe alongside the bedroom partition.

Pl. 99a—(Below left) A deteriorating example of an old cottage trunk.

Pl. 99b—(Below right) This decaying bedroom still shows signs of the original wall mortar.

(189) Gailey 1984, 140, 160.
(190) See the Cultra leaflet. Perhaps this positioning of the door originally facilitated the introduction of cattle into the cottage in the days of the 'byre-dwelling': Lysaght 1994, 11.
(191) Evans 1957, 45. He says that only the front door would have been in regular use, the back door being used mainly for avoiding draught problems, so that later, when chimney flues were added, these doors would have been blocked up or made into cupboards or windows. Pfeiffer and Shaffrey, on the other hand, comment that only one door was typical of Irish cottages, leading directly (or via a porch) into the kitchen (1990, 78, 83, 84). This seems to be the case in north Donegal. Aalen (1970, 41) speculates that, although the full significance of 'opposed doors' is not understood, 'it is hard to escape the conclusion' that they must be linked with the tradition of accommodating people and animals together in the same building. Ó Danachair (1964, 70) comes to the same conclusion.
(192) Evans 1957, 48.
(193) Gailey 1984, 133.
(194) *Ibid*. See also Evans 1957, 48 ('ever open door' and the half-door 'admitted most of the light').
(195) Evans 1957, 48.
(196) *Ibid*.
(197) Danaher (1975, 14) says that such lesser features in Irish cottages are 'neat and well-placed'.
(198) See Pfeiffer and Shaffrey 1990, 28.
(199) Evans (1957, 48) says that this was for constructional reasons and because glass was once expensive.
(200) Cf. Pfeiffer and Shaffrey 1990, 30, where it is claimed that rear windows are unusual in Irish cottages.
(201) For example, tiny two-sash types, with one pane top and bottom.
(202) Spacings were often dictated by 'norms as to size and numbers of windows suitable for lighting the various internal spaces' (Gailey 1984, 33).
(203) See e.g. Gailey 1984, 135 (later 'Georgian-style fenestration of the sliding-sash variety'); Pfeiffer and Shaffrey 1990, 114.
(204) Gailey 1984, 134; Pfeiffer and Shaffrey 1990, 107, 115.
(205) Gailey 1984, 135.
(206) *Ibid*.
(207) See generally Evans 1957, 45.
(208) *Ibid*., 48.
(209) See Gailey 1984, 77. In the Roshine area, for example, one cottage's oldest room to the right has both a window (front) and an interior connecting door blocked up with stones.
(210) See Pfeiffer and Shaffrey 1990, 8.
(211) For room sizes see p. 25 above.
(212) For discussion of the partitioning of a kitchen into a 'kitchen-bedroom' in the corner facing the door see McCourt 1965, 46.
(213) See the figures in Gailey 1984, 152.
(214) Gailey 1984, 164; as he says, stud-and-board partitions would not have been an original feature of an Irish cottage (*ibid*., 76).

Pl. 100—An outhouse by a cottage near Creeslough in which the floor is still lined with 'blue clay'.

Pl. 101—A typical flagstone floor in the kitchen of a north Donegal cottage.

Pl. 102—A surviving example of a 'candle lantern'.

(215)   *Ibid.*, 218.
(216)   *Ibid.*, 226 ('separation of members of the family').
(217)   Gailey (1984, 216) says that later subdivision into units (e.g. in the kitchen) gave 'sleeping or retiral space . . . for some of the family'. Evans (1957, 65) suggests that internal partitions 'probably' followed the adoption of the chimney flue as a contribution to privacy as well as comfort.
(218)   Gailey (1984, 148) comments that dressers and larger presses may initially have partitioned off a former byre end in the early 'byre-cottage'. He also says (*ibid.*, 216) that undifferentiated internal space was common in Irish cottages, and that any internal partitions were flimsy at best.
(219)   *Ibid.*, 209.
(220)   *Ibid.*, 78. Gailey points out that rigid ceilings, especially of timber sheeting, were inserted into many farmhouses in the latter part of the nineteenth century and later (*ibid.*, 209).
(221)   It is Gailey's view (1984, 224) that timber-sheeted ceilings may have constituted status symbols as well as being a practical improvement.
(222)   See Gailey 1984, 160.
(223)   Evans 1957, 45.
(224)   See e.g. Pfeiffer and Shaffrey 1990, 18 and 78. Gailey (1984, 218) comments that the development of upper-level sleeping as in loft floors led to the removal of beds from the kitchen, and Evans (1957, 69) suggests that a loft over part of the kitchen roof space may have begun as storage space before becoming a bedroom.
(225)   See generally McCourt 1970.
(226)   Gailey (1984, 130) mentions Irish half-lofts being usually over the end of the kitchen, lighted by a small gable window, with access by a ladder.
(227)   See Gailey 1984, 43.
(228)   *Ibid.*, 33 (kitchens tended to be 'square or slightly longer than wide') and 211.
(229)   *Ibid.*, 212.
(230)   *Ibid.*, 217.
(231)   Evans 1957, 59.
(232)   *Ibid.*, 59 ('a symbol of family continuity and of hospitality towards the stranger').
(233)   Gailey 1984, 213; Pfeiffer and Shaffrey 1990, 17.
(234)   Gailey 1984, 163.
(235)   *Ibid.*, 118.
(236)   *Ibid.*, 122.
(237)   Sometimes Donegal cottages have a simple local (non-slate) stone as lintel.
(238)   Pfeiffer and Shaffrey 1990, 23. Evans (1957, 59) points out that Irish cottage fires were usually at ground level because dry peat burns too quickly if the draught is strong.
(239)   Gailey 1984, 215.
(240)   See Gailey 1984, 224; Evans 1957, 63.
(241)   Evans (1957, 77) stresses that the 'fundamental fact in the geography of the Irish hearth' was the 'absence of the built-in oven'; but as Gailey (1984, 124) says, in the mid-nineteenth century firebars were being built and cast-iron ovens installed.

Pl. 103a—The 'street' in front of a long farmstead in Roshine.

Pl. 103b—A goose 'craw' set into the underside of steps up to a half-loft.

Pl. 103c—Part of a set of randomly sited farm buildings.

Pl. 103d—A row of farm buildings opposite a cottage (to left).

(242) See Gailey 1984, 122–3, 148–9.
(243) Cf. more generally Gailey 1984, 123, 151.
(244) *Ibid.*, 214–15.
(245) Pfeiffer and Shaffrey 1990, 11.
(246) Evans 1957, 68.
(247) *Ibid.*, 66.
(248) For example, in at least two Roshine cottages the crane upright is to the right of the fireplace.
(249) Gailey 1984, 215.
(250) *Ibid.*
(251) See e.g. Evans 1957, 65.
(252) See e.g. Evans 1957, 91 ('this was the most elaborate piece of furniture in the kitchen').
(253) See Gailey 1984, 213, 216.
(254) This lower part took pots and pans. Earlier examples had no cupboard doors at this level: see Gailey 1984, 216.
(255) See e.g. Gailey 1984, 216; Pfeiffer and Shaffrey 1990, 8, 10.
(256) Gailey 1984, 216.
(257) See e.g. Evans 1957, 88; Gailey 1984, 216 ('invariably placed against the front or rear wall and often it was not especially large'). Gailey also notes that in south Ulster a small table was hinged to the wall, occasionally in such a way that it 'could be set up at night to double as a shutter in front of the window opening'. One of the authors has seen just such an original table in a restored thatched cottage in County Fermanagh.
(258) See Evans 1957, 93 (the 'favourite fireside stool'). He also points out that low stools and benches allowed those sitting on them to avoid the smoke! See also Gailey 1984, 216.
(259) Evans (1957, 72) mentions that these were considered such vital pieces of equipment that they were clung on to even by those dispossessed during the Famine years.
(260) See Evans 1957, 93.
(261) *Ibid.*, 95–6.
(262) *Ibid.*, 97.
(263) See generally Gailey 1984, 217.
(264) See Evans 1957, 99 (such crosses placed above the door were thought to bring luck to the household).
(265) See Pfeiffer and Shaffrey 1990, 18.
(266) See generally Gailey 1984, 65.
(267) Such flooring was also commonly used in seasonal 'bothogs' in County Donegal, and the process of construction is described in Hannan and Bell 2000, 71, 79.
(268) See, more generally, Gailey 1984, 127.
(269) See Evans 1957, 89.
(270) *Ibid.*, 66.
(271) As Evans (1957, 40) says, '[s]anitation was of the crudest and closets unknown'.
(272) See Gailey 1984, 124, and his photos (at p. 236) of extended outhouses *at each end* of the dwelling.
(273) See Gailey 1984, 23; at pp 240–1 he cites a farm in the Strabane area where, when more room was needed, a new house was attached to the

Pl. 104—In this set of outhouses, the building in the foreground to the right has a chimney and fireplace, indicating that it was once used for boiling potatoes etc. for farm animals and possibly also for laundry purposes.

Pl. 105—A rare surviving example of a surface drain outside the kitchen door of a cottage in Dunfanaghy.

old one, and a door left between the old and new units: as conditions changed, the old portion could be used as a cattle byre and the connecting door closed up when necessary. Such converted use seems to have been not uncommon in the Dunfanaghy region. See also McCourt 1970, 13, 14 (the final separation of byre and dwelling came about when the lofted area 'was used as a barn which is reached from the yard by stone steps placed either against the sidewall beside the byre entrance or at the byre gable' (a 'byre-over-barn unit') and Gailey 1979, 130.

(274) See Evans 1957, 112.

(275) Evans (1957, 126) says that cavities were built in the thick walls of many old Irish farms as dog kennels or duck houses. In the case of one cottage in Roshine, such a feature was used as a goose house. Ó Danachair (1964, 60) describes fowl even being permitted to roost in various parts of a 'byre-house' kitchen, including the dresser!

(276) See Gailey 1984, 232; Pfeiffer and Shaffrey 1990, 19.

(277) Gailey 1984, 230. Aalen (1970, 34) notes that on the Donegal island of Gola the reconstructed longhouses were 'for hygienic reasons deliberately located on *sloping* sites and the byre ends were pointed down the slope' (emphasis added). Such positioning is also evident in some of the *old* remaining cottages on the mainland.

(278) See Evans 1957, 100.

(279) *Ibid.*, 101 ('massive stone gate piers', generally in the form of a conical-topped cylinder and kept whitewashed).

APPENDIX

Letter from one of the authors to *The Irish Times*, printed 5 October 1999

Sir,—Following on from the recent letters to your newspaper on rural development, there is another aspect I should like to raise which I consider to be even more serious than bad planning in the Irish countryside. It is the seemingly deliberate destruction of the old vernacular houses—be they cottages or crofts—throughout rural Ireland, but particularly on the Atlantic fringes.

Such old rural dwellings are still disappearing at an alarming rate month by month in a process encouraged by planning policies which seem to see no worth in them, as to my knowledge often the only way to achieve planning permission for a modern dwelling in scenic parts of the rural west and north-west is to undertake to demolish an existing old building and then build on its site. Thus, even as I write, old rural buildings which fit so naturally into the Irish rural landscape are being pulled down to make way for 'bungalow blitz' replacements or worse. Yet such old buildings, with official government encouragement, could so easily, with modern techniques, be preserved and be brought up to modern standards, as is done in most other European countries.

I have seen this phenomenon sweeping parts of rural Co. Donegal which I know well. When I bought my old 'croft' some 30 years ago there (sadly now one of the few examples left in my area), whitewashed vernacular buildings, roofed in the aesthetically pleasing, locally–mined slates, were everywhere to be seen and were being lived in. Now hardly any remain. Most have been bulldozed, with the full approval—and indeed encouragement—of officialdom to make a 'site' for what is often a modern monstrosity, or have been left to decay in the background of the house, possibly as an extra cattle byre on a farm.

This 'policy' (if such it can be called) must be reversed immediately to save what few examples of traditional vernacular buildings still remain in the scenic parts of Ireland. Ironically, in my experience it is often non-national 'blow-ins' who appreciate this wonderful part of the Irish heritage and are restoring such old buildings in the traditional style. Unless something positive is done about this problem at a high official level—and quickly—it is bound to have an effect on tourism. For once foreign tourists find that the cottages which still feature on postcards hardly now exist in Ireland, they may well decide not to come back.

As with the Irish donkey, the time is fast approaching when the only way a tourist can see a traditional Irish cottage is to buy a postcard!

Yours, etc,

Dr Clive Symmons